# PETER MALINS'
# ROSE BOOK

# The Rose Arc

ESTELLE K. GERARD

# PETER MALINS' ROSE BOOK

## Peter Malins
### AND
## M. M. Graff

*Illustrated with fifty-five
photographs*

**DODD, MEAD & COMPANY**
**NEW YORK**

Unless otherwise indicated, photographs are by M. M. Graff.

1    2    3    4    5    6    7    8    9    10

**Library of Congress Cataloging in Publication Data**

Malins, Peter.
  Peter Malins' Rose book.

  Includes index.
  1. Roses.  2. Rose culture.  I.  Graff, M. M., joint
author.  II.  Title.  III.  Title.
SB411.M366      635.9′33′372      79-13889
ISBN 0-396-07716-1

# Contents

# Acknowledgments

The authors extend their warm thanks to Dr. George S. Avery, Jr., Director Emeritus of the Brooklyn Botanic Garden, who first suggested the writing of this book; to the staff of the BBG Library, Marie G. Giasi and Anna Reddy, for resourceful guidance in research; to William A. Warriner for invaluable information on the incidence of pelargonidin in roses; to Edith C. Schurr for her resolute and successful campaign to secure plants of 'Eva' for the rose garden; and to Frank J. Bowman, Daphne Drury, Estelle K. Gerard and Janis Klavins for supplying essential photographs.

# Introduction

Many thousands of people from all over the world visit the Cranford Rose Garden at Brooklyn Botanic Garden each year. A gift of Mr. and Mrs. Walter V. Cranford, the Rose Garden was constructed in June, 1927. An engineer who contracted to build the Brooklyn portion of the New York Subway System, Mr. Cranford was a shy man who chanced to learn that Dr. Gager, the Botanic Garden's first Director, was seeking a donor for what was to become a great public rose garden.

Harold A. Caparn, one of the foremost landscape architects of the time, was selected to design the Rose Garden. Mr. Caparn divided the 500-foot-long area by erecting a latticework pavilion on a rectangular terrace extending across the 93-foot-wide Rose Garden, a fine vantage point to view the longer northern rectangle of newer hybrids as well as the shorter area devoted to old and species roses.

In 1935, in memory of her late husband, Mrs. Cranford underwrote the construction of an attractive extension, the Rose Arc and Reflecting Pool, also designed by Mr. Caparn.

The Cranford family's interest in the Rose Garden continued throughout Mrs. Cranford's lifetime and that of her daughter, Margaret, until the latter's death in 1974.

In 1977 rosarians from many parts of the country came to celebrate the 50th Anniversary of the Cranford Rose Garden and enjoyed, with Botanic Garden members and friends, the vibrant colors and fragrances of more than 5,000 rose bushes.

Among the visitors to the Rose Garden are artists, photographers, children with parents or teachers, and many bridal parties as well as home gardeners in search of names of varieties for their own grounds. Informal talks are given on specially designated Rose Days in June and September each year. The talks and demonstrations of methods of rose care are given by Peter Malins who has been chief rosarian of the Rose Garden since 1960. The flourishing condition of the Rose Garden is a tribute to Mr. Malins' knowledge, energy, skill and dedication to his chosen flower.

Elizabeth Scholtz, *Director*
Brooklyn Botanic Garden

# 1
# The Origin of Modern Roses

Roses are the most ancient plant grown primarily for pleasure, though some species were credited with medicinal properties and others were employed in religious ceremonies. The earliest known depiction of roses in a garden is in frescos painted on the walls of a house near the Minoan palace at Cnossos, Crete, where civilization reached its peak in 2000 B.C.

It is believed that the remote ancestors of our modern roses originated in western Asia, chiefly in Persia, the Caucasus and Syria. Seafaring Greeks and Phoenicians distributed these wild roses throughout the Mediterranean countries. Roman legions carried the Dog Briar, *Rosa canina*, from its origin in the eastern Mediterranean to Britain where it became so widely naturalized that many consider it a native. Armies included rosebushes in their baggage not for aesthetic reasons but for medicine. The Dog Briar takes its name from the supposed ability of its root to counteract the bite of a rabid dog, while according to a durable but wholly unfounded

1

belief, a conserve of rose petals was thought to cure tuberculosis.

The Moslem invasions of the seventh and eighth centuries were also instrumental in distributing species roses from western Asia. Roses from captured Persia were introduced to Spain and gradually spread through most of Europe. It is thought that Crusaders returning from Palestine may also have transported roses to France and Britain.

When species roses from widely separated geographical regions were brought together in gardens, they were able to crossbreed, producing hybrids that could never have occurred in their native sites. Pollination was effected at random by insects, so determination of the probable bloodlines that went into any particular strain of roses is not much more than speculation.

In addition to collecting natural hybrids, rose growers improved their stock by selecting and propagating specimens with extra doubling, exceptionally intense fragrance or unusual color breaks such as striping and marbling. Despite these early efforts, for many centuries the garden rose had a limited range of color from white through various shades of pink and rose to crimson, violet and purple. The majority flowered only once though Virgil praised a rose that had a "double spring," that is, a second flowering in autumn.

In the first decades of the nineteenth century, rose breeding was given new impetus by Empress Josephine's passionate addiction to her beloved flower. In addition to collecting existing roses for her unsurpassed garden at Malmaison, she stimulated an extensive program of growing roses from seed and was in this way a pioneer in the art of modern rose breeding.

The importation of a collection of cultivated roses from

China and the rediscovery of an Asian species in Austria were prime factors in the breeding revolution that produced our modern roses. Half-a-dozen varieties of the China Rose, *Rosa chinensis*, were imported to England, France and the Netherlands in the last quarter of the eighteenth century. Their colors included blush, pink, red and yellow. Their light fragrance resembled that of the chests in which tea was shipped from the Orient. It was so distinct from the heavy perfume of the familiar Damasks, Gallicas and Albas that it earned its bearers the name of Tea-Scented Chinas. Both the name and the scent are inherited by their progeny, the Tea Roses and our modern Hybrid Teas. The China Rose is a delicate plant with slender twigs, small, loosely formed flowers and the priceless gift of continual bloom, a major contribution even when balanced against a loss of fragrance and hardiness.

The second revolutionary factor was the rediscovery of *Rosa foetida* and its variety, *R. f. bicolor*. It is conjectured that these roses originated in Turkey and Persia and were carried to Spain by the invading Moslems. From there they were distributed across Europe, but gradually died out except where they had naturalized in Austria, a circumstance that gives them their misleading names of Austrian Yellow and Austrian Copper. These little five-petaled flowers are distinguished by their intense and unique color. The first is a brilliant chrome yellow with a glossy finish; the second, a rather harsh orange with yellow on the reverse. The potent blood of these little wildings is responsible for one segment of the magnificent range of color and pattern in modern roses: cream, yellow, cantaloupe, peach, orange, salmon and scarlet, both in pure tones and in blends and bicolors. Again there is a price: *Rosa foetida* is excessively prone to blackspot and mildew and its name translates as "stinking"; so we gain glorious colors at the cost of reduced disease resistance and further diminution of fragrance.

There is no question, as evidenced by sales of rosebushes and by the preference of visitors to the Brooklyn Botanic Garden (BBG) rose garden, that rose lovers choose brilliance, clarity and variety of color over all other considerations. Gradually the soberly colored Hybrid Perpetuals (mostly once-blooming, despite their bragging title) in the center beds have been replaced by modern Grandifloras and Floribundas, though the powerfully scented old-fashioned roses are still preserved along the flanking fences. This may be a good solution for home gardeners: grow the dazzling modern roses for display and cut flowers but make room in a shrub border for some of the intoxicatingly perfumed types such as the recent repeat-blooming Hybrid Rugosas, the dainty Moss Roses and the Damasks and Gallicas, cherished for centuries as the source of attar of roses.

# 2
# Classification of Roses

Garden roses fall into five main classes: bush roses, standard or tree roses, miniatures, shrub roses and climbers.

## BUSH ROSES

Bush roses seldom grow over six feet tall and need no support. They are divided into five classes according to plant habit and type of bloom.

1. *Hybrid Perpetual* (HP). In the early decades of the nineteenth century, this new race of hardy, vigorous roses was created by crossing the everblooming but tender *Rosa chinensis* with sturdy shrub roses such as Damasks. The epithet "Perpetual" is a seller's hyperbole: of 83 HPs listed in Bobbink & Atkins' 1940 catalogue, only 40 are marked with an *R* to denote repeat blooming. Most HPs are rich in old-rose perfume (the white 'Frau Karl Druschki' is an exception) and produce

5

immensely full flowers in a range of color from white and pink to rose-red, crimson and violet. HPs were the preeminent garden rose from the 1840s to the late 1890s when they were superseded by the more brilliantly colored Hybrid Teas.

2. *Hybrid Tea* (HT). The first Hybrid Tea, the silvery pink 'La France,' was raised in 1867 by crossing a Hybrid Perpetual with a Tea Rose whose parents included *Rosa chinensis.* About 1900, infusions of Austrian Yellow and Austrian Copper blood revolutionized garden rose breeding and produced our modern Hybrid Teas. In the best forms, the bud is urn-shaped. This high-standing center, tight in the waist and flaring at the lip, should persist as the outer petals slowly unfold in a graceful spiral. HTs may be tea scented or have a fresh, somewhat fruity odor but few have the rich perfume associated with old shrub roses. When a HT is described as "fragrant," it should be remembered that this means "fragrant for a HT." HTs are superlative as cut flowers but their somewhat rangy, angular bushes have little decorative value in the garden. They are not reliably hardy in very cold climates and their disease-prone foliage requires frequent spraying. However, their unchallenged popularity indicates that gardeners think the result is worth whatever effort is called for.

3. *Polyantha* (Pol.). The first of these low-growing, everblooming roses was produced in 1868 by crossing the Japanese *Rosa multiflora* with one of the forms of *R. chinensis,* the Dwarf Pink China. The small flowers, often with crinkled petals, were borne in tight clusters and much resembled those of Ramblers. In their turn, these rather stunted-looking plants with their limited color range were supplanted by the larger, brighter and

showier Floribundas. 'Cécile Brunner' (1880) is the only Polyantha likely to be remembered, and then partly because of its appealing nickname, the Sweetheart Rose.

4. *Floribunda* (FL). In 1924 the Danish rose breeder Svend Poulsen crossed Polyanthas with Hybrid Teas to found a new race of roses with clusters of medium-sized flowers. These came to be known as Floribundas. The chief value of Floribundas is their profusion of bloom throughout the entire season. The form of individual flowers is usually less important than the impact of their massed color. They are unequalled for landscape effect: the taller ones make excellent hedges while the dwarfer ones are suitable for the forefront of shrub borders. If you think of them as everblooming azaleas, you will find the right place for them. Floribundas look their best when planted in generous groups of a single variety, not as isolated specimens or in mixtures.

5. *Grandiflora* (GR). This is an artificial classification based on size rather than on a new combination of bloodlines. Grandifloras are essentially tall Floribundas with spreading clusters of flowers resembling those of Hybrid Teas, or so the advertisers claim. Because of their height, Grandifloras don't fit snugly into the landscape as Floribundas do, while the individual flowers are usually too short stemmed for cutting. The fact that the nearly identical 'Queen Elizabeth' and 'Gene Boerner' are classed respectively as Grandiflora and Floribunda indicates that the classification is inexact and of little help in guiding prospective buyers. Grandifloras are not recognized as a class by The Royal National Rose Society of Britain. The term is used in this book only to aid gardeners in locating a desired variety in catalogues that still use this outmoded classification.

## STANDARD OR TREE ROSES

Tree roses are created by grafting buds of a selected rose variety onto a tall trunk of sturdy stock, usually a Rugosa. Tree roses are an invaluable means of offsetting the flatness of beds of conventional bush roses. In addition, they offer bouquets at eye and nose level, a boon to rose lovers with ailing backs. It must be noted, however, that although the trunk is hardy, the head requires protection in cold climates. Methods of safeguarding tree roses are detailed on pages 216–219.

## MINIATURE ROSES

Miniature roses are 6 to 15 inches high with small double flowers, wiry stems and delicate foliage. In many respects they resemble *Rosa chinensis*. They are in excellent scale for rock gardens, edges of borders, window boxes and containers. Like all roses, they must be given plenty of room for air circulation, not crammed in among other plants. Miniature roses would be sadly out of scale in the BBG rose garden whose three sections comprise well over an acre. Readers who want information are advised to consult books specializing in this class. *The Complete Book of Miniature Roses* by Charles Marden Fitch (Hawthorn Books, 1977) is comprehensive and clearly written from firsthand experience.

## OLD ROSES AND SHRUB ROSES

Most of the ancient roses bloom only once. Some of their names are familiar through association with history, religion and romance: 'Rosa Mundi'; *Rosa hugonis;* the York and Lancaster Rose; *Rosa centifolia,* the fat cabbage rose lovingly depicted by Dutch and Flemish painters; and *Rosa alba,* the white rose used symbolically in religious paintings. Many of the old roses— Damasks, Gallicas, Moss Roses, Albas, Musks and Rugosas—are ravishingly fragrant. Modern hybrids of these old roses retain the heady scent and add the merit of repeat blooming. Since shrub roses vary greatly in height, spread and character of flowers, it is well to study them in a large collection before making a choice.

## CLIMBING ROSES

1. *Ramblers* (R). These are in effect climbing Polyanthas with tight clusters of small flowers produced on canes of the current year. The names 'Bloomfield Courage,' 'Dorothy Perkins' and 'Tausendschon' may be familiar. Ramblers have dropped from popularity because most bloom only once and the entire plant—leaves and flowers alike—is apt to be gray with mildew despite conscientious spraying. To demonstrate how rapidly a class of roses will be discarded when superior forms are developed, look at the listing of 59 Ramblers in the 1940 Bobbink & Atkins catalogue. In 1957, the same firm offered just two.

2. *Large-flowered Climbers* (LFC). These bloom on canes two to three years old and so must be pruned sparingly—a problem, as some of the old varieties are rampant growers. Since most of them—'Dr. W. Van Fleet,' 'Silver Moon' and 'Dr. Huey'—bloom only once, it is questionable whether they repay the room their exuberant growth demands. 'Dr. W. Van Fleet' has been

replaced by its sport 'New Dawn' which produces its delicate silvery pink flowers all season. Among the more recent once-flowering climbers are the vigorous clean-foliaged 'Elegance' with primrose-yellow flowers of perfect HT form, and the white 'City of York.' Repeat bloomers include the overused 'Blaze' (crimson fading to carmine) and 'Golden Showers' with large, loosely formed flowers of deep yellow quickly fading to cream. Climbers conserve precious garden space as they take to the air on fences, trellises or arbors. The production of hardy repeat-flowering climbers presents a splendid opportunity to alert breeders. Gardeners will eagerly welcome varieties that offer lavish quantities of well-formed flowers yet occupy a minimum of growing room.

3. *Climbing Hybrid Teas* (CL HT). In the South, these tall-growing sports of Hybrid Teas make spectacular displays, flowering on canes that persist from year to year. In more severe climates, the long canes tend to winter-kill: they are obviously no hardier than their normal HT parents. They may in fact be more prone to winter damage since they are trained on fences or trellises, exposed to the full sweep of freezing winds, whereas their parents grow closer to the ground and may benefit by windbreaks such as walls, hedges or shrubbery. Since flowers are produced on canes at least one year old, it follows that production of bloom is curtailed if these canes, or a large portion of their length, are winter-killed. The plant may spend all its energy in replacing the lost canes instead of developing flower buds. Climbing HTs can be protected by untying the canes, laying them on the ground and covering them with earth. If this seems too much bother, select climbers of known hardiness even if their flowers are not up to HT standards.

4. *Trailers.* Trailing roses are tall-growing varieties

with exceptionally flexible canes. They are chiefly used to cover banks, as a soil-holding ground cover or planted at the top of a retaining wall to drape its face. Trailing roses have been dropped from most catalogues and you must turn to growers specializing in old roses to find onetime favorites such as 'Max Graf,' 'Little Compton Creeper' or species like *Rosa wichuraiana* and our native Prairie Rose, *R. setigera,* whose lax canes can be pegged down to make a cover for rough hillsides and to provide shelter and food for wildlife.

# 3
# Selecting Roses

Before you plunge into the seductive pages of catalogues, you should consider some mundane factors beyond the pictured charm of a flower. Since roses don't float unsupported in air like cherubs, it is important to assess the vigor of the plant that produces them. This can best be determined by visiting a botanic garden or other large collection. If you want, for instance, a light pink rose, jot down the names of the varieties that best suit your taste. Then make a second survey, this time looking for straight necks, strong thick canes and clean foliage. Plants with weak twiggy canes and those showing excessive amounts of blackspot or mildew are at once eliminated. In sifting out the remaining candidates, look for fragrance, profusion of bloom, unfading color and grace of form in the full-blown flower. The rose that earns the highest rating in all respects will give you lasting satisfaction.

Since Hybrid Teas are one of the very few flowers that look better in a vase than on the plant, you should direct your selection towards colors that harmonize with your indoor decorative scheme. For instance, if your draperies or rug or upholstery fabrics are in shades of candy pink, rose, burgundy or lilac, don't buy the hot orange-coral 'Tropicana.' Conversely, if your decorative scheme features shrimp, coral, vermilion or scarlet, 'Tropicana' will be a stunning accent but true rose-pink, crimson or magenta flowers will look dowdy. In a word, if you make a firm choice between tints and shades of orange-red and purple-red, you will avoid jarring clashes both in the house and in the garden. In very large gardens, the warring colors can be separated by a buffer of white or yellow roses. In a small plot which can all be seen at one glance, it is better to concentrate on either the orange or the purple side of red on the color wheel.

As mentioned earlier, Floribundas are grown chiefly for mass effect, not for individual blooms, though there are notable exceptions as there are to any statement made about living plants. Floribundas should be planted in generous drifts of one variety—not fewer than three plants and preferably more. These are landscape plants for hedges or the front of a shrub border. If planted in a mixture of varieties, they will give an unpleasantly spotty, unstable effect. Similarly bouquets of HTs are most appealing when composed of one variety, so again a minimum of three plants of a variety should be grouped to insure a sufficient selection of flowers for cutting.

If you are going to invest in roses in multiples of three or more, you want to be very sure that you choose the best available in the desired color, not alone for beauty of flowers but also for vigor of growth, profusion of bloom and disease resistance. These are facts you can seldom determine from catalogues, especially if the rose is deficient in one or more respects. First, every breeder thinks his goose is a swan; second, roses that win high acclaim under one set of climatic conditions may languish in another.

The best way to choose roses is to study them in a botanic garden, nursery or large public or private collection near your locality. The studio portraits of roses in catalogues show them at their moment of perfection but give no hint of how the rose will perform under garden conditions. Some roses—the well-loved 'Peace' is one of them—mature gracefully, retaining their beauty until the petals drop. Others, while charming on first opening, age poorly: their petals may droop or reflex in sharp points (a fault called quilling) or develop disfiguring spots or streaks; the color may fade or change disagreeably; the neck may be too weak to support the flower especially when weighted by rain. These defects will be clearly evident in a botanic garden at a time when shortage of manpower prevents the removal of blooms that have passed their prime.

It is advisable to visit the display garden not only in the peak of early June bloom but also in midsummer when you can check to see how your tentative choices perform in hot weather. Since all the roses in the garden receive the same spray routine, you can readily assess the degree of disease resistance. Some varieties will be clean foliaged while others are nearly defoliated, with the remaining leaves marred by blackspot or mildew.

Another advantage of visiting a botanic garden is the opportunity to study and assess the so-called test roses, distributed by the introducers under the number by which the cross was recorded. Presumably the roses are tentatively submitted for evaluation by the rosarian. However, in twenty years of experience at the BBG, no test rose, regardless of how adversely it was criticized, has failed to be introduced the following year. The practical purpose of a test garden is to provide early exposure of a new rose. The hope is that it will attract the favorable attention of the rose-buying public, thus inviting orders as soon as the rose is introduced under a glamorous name. New roses are usually named by the hybridizer or, in the case of a foreign-bred rose, by the introducer. This is entirely reasonable: it is doubtful that rose growers would rush to buy 'Duftwolke' which certainly has more appeal under its translated name of 'Fragrant Cloud.'

For those without access to a rose collection, the following chapters will evaluate some of the most widely grown varieties and those seldom listed despite outstanding merit. Many of these roses have received the AARS award (All-American Rose Selection) given to new varieties after two years of testing in rose gardens in different regions of the country. In theory, an AARS award should guarantee a vigorous plant with flowers of exhibition quality.

This is far from being the case. The explanation may lie in the fact that a great majority of rose breeders and commercial growers are located on the West Coast, chiefly in California and Oregon. When roses have been evaluated on the basis of their performance in this ideal climate, it is understandable that some may falter when subjected to oppressive heat, stagnant air and high humidity—conditions not uncommon in New York City summers. One such failure is the HT 'Oregold' (AARS 1975) which dies back in summer, puts out a few grotesquely large flowers on the surviving six inches of canes in fall and then usually winter-kills. It seems evident that judging is far too limited geographically and that more reports—and more candid reports—are needed from growers in areas other than the West Coast.

The awarding of prizes to roses with serious defects is harder to condone, especially when the flaws seem to be inherent rather than the result of adverse climatic conditions. How could 'Gene Boerner' (AARS 1969) have been chosen when its pleasant pink complexion develops magenta streaks and blotches as it matures? 'Medallion' (AARS 1973) is a unique cantaloupe color, but its huge shaggy flowers nod on weak necks especially when rain soaked. The fire-orange Floribunda 'Bahia' (AARS 1974) fades soon after opening to gray-white: its clusters look like crepe paper Halloween decorations that have been caught in a cloudburst.

Perhaps in these years there was no really flawless rose among the candidates. In that case it would have been better to give no award at all than to deceive gardeners by praising introductions which in fact had grave demerits. It is regrettable that AARS awards can't be regarded as impartial or free of commercialism. Choosing your roses under actual growing conditions is still the best insurance of satisfaction, even if it entails a journey to a botanic garden or large rose collection.

Despite the cataloguer's compulsive search for novelties, "new" doesn't necessarily mean "better." 'Peace,' introduced in 1945, still outsells all other varieties, while 'Tropicana,' 1963, is crowding it closely for popularity. The following lists therefore include some older roses of enduring merit and also some the authors feel have missed the recognition they deserve, at least based on their performance in the Brooklyn Botanic Garden.

A word on color terminology: in 1950, the introduction of 'Independence' gave rose growers an entirely new dimension of color, a combination of pigments not found on any color chart, without a name and impossible to reproduce even with the finest color printing. The advent of pelargonidin, the orange-red pigment that gives 'Independence' its dazzling brilliance, has resulted in an astonishing new race of roses in which a carmine base is overlaid with a translucent wash of orange which varies in depth and intensity with each variety. The two colors are not mixed but retain their separate identity. Their interplay creates a vibrant quality that highlights them across a garden. Because of their uncanny Dayglo effect, these roses will dominate any planting, a factor that should be taken into consideration when choosing companion roses.

Many of these orange-carmine roses have a defect: the orange overtone fades as the flowers age. The effect is especially distressing in cluster flowers when the older central flower turns magenta in a ring of orange-red youngsters, as is the case with 'Independence.' Once again, the reader is urged to study roses in a collection, under actual growing conditions, to determine which varieties fade and which preserve their glowing color to the last.

# 4

# Hybrid Tea Roses

A long and intensive study of the 900 varieties of roses grown in the Brooklyn Botanic Garden leads to the conclusion that the most enduring plants, those with strong constitutions and luminous clear-colored flowers, trace their pedigree to two patriarchs: 'Crimson Glory' (1935) and 'Eva' (1933). Both were bred by the late Wilhelm Kordes whose memory will be held in honor by generations of rose lovers. 'Crimson Glory' and its glowing offspring 'Charlotte Armstrong' (1940) and 'Chrysler Imperial' (1950) were prolific parents of red, deep rose and rose-pink roses, mainly Hybrid Teas. 'Proud Land,' 'Mister Lincoln,' 'Hallmark,' 'Perfume Delight,' 'Queen Elizabeth' and 'Firelight,' among hundreds of others, all trace their lineage to one of the royal pair named above.

'Eva' is an enigmatic Hybrid Musk described as a pillar rose with white-centered, carmine-red flowers. This seems an unlikely source for the innovative salmon, shrimp-pink and orange roses that flowed in an iridescent stream from 'Eva.' 'Pinocchio,' 'Fashion,' 'Spartan,' 'Circus,' 'City of Belfast,' 'Montezuma' and 'Contempo' are outstanding roses that owe their distinctive coloring and clarity to 'Eva's' potent blood.

Since most of 'Eva's' descendants are Floribundas, they will appear in the following chapter. However, the influence of this unassuming rose weaves itself with telling effect into Hybrid Teas as well. It must be remembered that 'Eva's' grandchild, 'Baby Chateau' (1936), when mated with 'Crimson Glory,' produced the incendiary 'Independence' in 1943. This was the orange-over-carmine pelargonidin-carrying rose that sparked a revolution in rose breeding.

'Peace' should be included in the list of dependable parents even though it is not a blood relation of the patriarchs. It has produced a number of sports as well as being the parent of some admirable roses to which— with the one exception of 'Sterling Silver'—it has transmitted its stalwart constitution.

It is proposed, then, that inheritance of the blood of the patriarchs, 'Crimson Glory' and 'Eva,' with 'Peace' as a significant collaborator, carries with it insurance of health, vigor and luminous colors. Roses that share this distinguished ancestry will be noted so that they can be compared with those that lack it. If independent studies bear out this theory, it will be a valuable guide to choosing roses that embody permanence as well as beauty.

## RED HYBRID TEAS

The most fragrant modern roses are red ones. The reason is simple: unlike the yellows, salmons and oranges, their ancestral old-rose perfume has not been diluted by admixture with blood of the scentless or ill-smelling *Rosa foetida.* Red Hybrid Teas have a second and perhaps more important distinction: they are the only class in which a good number of recent introductions are indisputably superior to those produced in the 40s and 50s.

**Crimson Glory** (1935) was for years the standard by which other red roses were judged. It has fragrant, deep garnet flowers with a velvety blackish bloom, borne on low-spreading bushes with an excessive attraction for mildew. It is now showing signs of diminished vigor, not at all surprising in view of its age, but will live triumphantly in its many illustrious descendants.

**Chrysler Imperial** ('Charlotte Armstrong' x 'Mirandy,' 1952) is one of 'Crimson Glory's' most famous offspring, extensively used in breeding and still a worthy rose in its own right. The plant is tall and rather spindly, with too few canes and too much mildew. Flowers are beautifully formed with high centers and are intensely fragrant. The color is rosy crimson, somewhat lighter than 'Crimson Glory': it fades to a distressing magenta with age.

**Red Masterpiece** (1974) has 'Chrysler Imperial' as grandparent on both sides. It is a velvety dark red, full-petaled flower of great substance. A rather stubby bud opens into a loose mass of petals which quill and recurve sharply. The fragrance is slight. Flowers have a tendency to ball and are sometimes too heavy for their supporting stems.

**John S. Armstrong** ('Charlotte Armstrong' x seedling, 1961) is classed as a Grandiflora but is actually lower in stature than most HTs. The mid-sized flowers are loosely formed, attractively ruffled and deep rose-red. The plant is vigorous with a constantly renewed stock of sturdy maroon canes clothed with foliage to the ground. There

**Chrysler Imperial.** Among its distinguished descendants are 'Hallmark,' 'Mister Lincoln,' 'Proud Land,' 'American Home' and 'Oklahoma.'

is a tendency to mildew, a weakness shared by most red roses, but this is not serious enough to cause defoliation if a routine spraying program is faithfully carried out.

**Hallmark** ('Independence' x 'Chrysler Imperial,' 1966). Interestingly, the breeding of this rose repeats the original magic combination of 'Crimson Glory' and 'Eva' but several steps lower on the family tree. The plant has tremendously strong canes with dense, dull-surfaced, disease-resistant leaves. It is a free bloomer, producing many stubby buds which open to very full, cup-shaped blossoms with a mass of short petals in the center. The young flower is rose-red; deep, but with a compelling light-reflective quality. In maturity it fades to rose bengal, well on the purple side of crimson. The fragrance is rich old-rose with a curious, quite pleasant musky undertone.

**Red Chief** (seedling x 'Chrysler Imperial,' 1967) is the best long-established red rose in the BBG, as it combines all the excellences of vigor, fragrance, good form, and profuse and continual bloom. It is a tall plant with canes that are nearly uniform in height so that all the flowers are presented at the same level for maximum impact. The flowers are velvety crimson with good form and a long-lasting high center. The plant is apparently indifferent to heat as it blooms all summer with the utmost generosity. The flowers fade from crimson to rose-red and end as a rather jarring magenta. However, due to the lavish production of bloom, aging blossoms can be snipped off without diminishing the flowery effect. The flowers are delectably scented with a combination of heavy old-rose fragrance and a substantial undertone of fruitcake well laced with brandy. 'Red Chief' has disappeared from all the catalogues we were able to consult. It is perhaps handicapped by the banality of its name which does it less than justice. We hope to persuade some rose nurseries to reinstate it, a service to gardeners for which the BBG will be happy to supply budwood.

**Mister Lincoln** ('Chrysler Imperial' x 'Charles Mallerin,' AARS 1962) is the full, heavily scented crimson rose traditionally favored by male gardeners. On the basis of sound constitution and lavish production of flowers in June, it is among the finest red HTs in the BBG. Its flowers start out with the classic high-centered form but quickly open into an exuberance of velvety petals which recurve with age until they touch the stem, giving the mature flower the globular shape of a football chrysanthemum. Some petals may be streaked with white but this is not prevalent enough to be disfiguring. 'Mister Lincoln,' in its profusion of petals and rich heady perfume, resembles a Hybrid Perpetual and is, in modern dress, what most people mean when they speak of a cabbage rose.

**Proud Land** ('Chrysler Imperial' x red seedling, 1969) is in close contention with 'Mister Lincoln' for top honors among commercially available red roses. The bud is pure blood red, passing to crimson as the flower ages. The color is deep but has a brilliant intensity with great carrying power: it draws the eye from a distance. In cool weather the flowers have an uncanny glow of cyclamen purple. 'Proud Land' is so charged with vigor that it tends to grow too tall. Flowers can be cut with three-foot stems. If left on the plant, the canes of spent flowers should be cut back quite severely in order to bring the next blooms down to nose level where their intense fragrance can be enjoyed without use of a stepladder.

'Proud Land' is a magnificent plant, far more free in its bloom than 'Mister Lincoln,' and is the cause of a difference of opinion between the authors. While both agree that 'Red Chief' is the best red rose of previous years, they are divided as to which is second best. One author thinks 'Mister Lincoln' has better form but gives 'Proud Land' high marks for garden decoration, citing its lavish nonstop bloom. The other favors 'Proud Land' as 'Mister Lincoln' is apt to sulk in summer, and what's the use of good form if a rose doesn't bloom?

The division was healed by compromise. In September of 1978, **Royal Canadian** (parentage uncertain,

Scarlet Knight.

1969) summoned its forces and produced buds and flowers of breathtaking quality. The color is deep blood red
without a trace of blue: it remains clear and unfading
until petal drop. The form is exemplary, with a long-
lasting high spiral center, ample petals, velvety finish
and rich fragrance. The plant glistens with vitality: it has
dense leathery foliage and thumb-thick canes. 'Royal
Canadian' has performed a valuable service: since the
authors agree that this is one of the finest red Hybrid
Teas ever bred, they are back in harmony again.

The rose that comes nearest to spectrum scarlet is ap-
propriately named **Scarlet Knight** ('Happiness' x 'Inde-

pendence,' 1966). Undoubtedly it gets its clear color from 'Independence,' the child of 'Eva' that brought Dayglo orange into the rose bed. 'Scarlet Knight' is listed as a Grandiflora, that purely artificial class invented as a sales gimmick and often, as in this case, completely misleading. 'Scarlet Knight' is not taller than the average HT and bears its flowers singly. It has anything but classic form, being flat as a zinnia when fully open, but it is a steady producer even in the sultriest part of the summer. The flowers are clear blood red and have a slight but agreeable scent. The neatly imbricated petals might be cut from panne velvet; their delicately rippled margins create a fascinating play of highlight and shadow. Best of all, the flowers of 'Scarlet Knight' are extraordinarily lasting on the plant. They age gracefully, darkening in tone but not turning magenta as many reds do. Despite its unconventional shape and a regrettable tendency to mildew, 'Scarlet Knight' was voted the most favored red rose in an informal poll of visitors to the BBG.

Two red-and-white roses of novel color pattern were introduced in the past year. One of them, **Double Delight,** won the AARS award for 1977. 'Double Delight' has a share of patriarchal blood: one of its parents, 'Garden Party,' is a cross between 'Charlotte Armstrong' and 'Peace.' 'Double Delight' has buds that agree with their catalogue portrait in having broad bands of cherry red on an ivory to light yellow ground. The bud form is soon lost: the flower opens quite flat and is of variable color. Some are almost entirely white with just a thin line of red around the petal edges. In others, the dark color spreads over the whole flower, darkening as it goes, ending as a dingy magnolia purple color for which a rich old-rose fragrance is not sufficient compensation. Some gardeners are apparently willing to give garden room to a rose purely for the sake of its bud. This must be so or else 'Eclipse' would long ago have borne out its name and lapsed into oblivion. However, the majority opinion is summed up in a visitor's comment: "I bought 'Double Delight' and I was *so* disappointed with it!"

**Snowfire** ('Detroiter' x 'Liberty Bell,' 1973) the other new red-and-white rose, was greeted with astonishment and delight when it first flowered in the BBG in 1977. The deep rose-red interior made a striking contrast with the white reverse. Petals were thick and opaque with a suedelike surface, so dense that neither color showed through on the other side. Canes were exceptionally prickly, but this fierce armament was no protection against overwhelming mildew or the inherent infirmity that caused the plants to die back inch by inch until by fall the living canes were mere stubs. It is hoped that the breeder will persevere in the effort to put a strong plant under this extraordinarily effective color break.

Visitors to the BBG often ask if we have a black rose. None exists and it's doubtful that one would be admired, except perhaps made up of velvet as an ornament for a dowager's Sunday hat. The deepest red is **Oklahoma** ('Chrysler Imperial' x 'Charles Mallerin,' 1964). 'Oklahoma' is a sultry dark garnet, made even gloomier by purple-brown shadings in the depths. Because of the saturated color and matt finish, the flowers are so little light-reflective that they tend to merge with the foliage and may be overlooked unless you are standing close by. The plant is vigorous and upright with stems strong enough to support the heavy flowers. Because of their full petalage, flowers may ball in hot weather. This is a distressing and unsightly affliction whereby the outer petals of a bud become glued together, locking across the top. The flower swells at the base but, being effectually sealed, is unable to open and ends up falling off in a sodden discolored ball.

**American Home** ('Chrysler Imperial' x 'New Yorker,' 1960) is another deep garnet rose but, being a trifle lighter and more light-gathering than 'Oklahoma,' gives a better account of itself in the garden. The huge flowers, breathing a powerful perfume, are carried on strong hardy canes.

For those who like their red roses with a good dash of cerise or purple, there are few but good choices. **Charlotte Armstrong** ('Soeur Thérèse' x 'Crimson Glory,' AARS 1941) takes pride of place both for glowing color and for a list of illustrious progeny. 'Chrysler Imperial,' 'Queen Elizabeth,' 'Helen Traubel,' 'Tiffany' and 'Mojave' are a sampling. 'Charlotte Armstrong' is Junoesque, the term used to describe a queenly woman of ample endowment. The bud is long and graceful: it opens into a solidly filled flower of peony form, measuring a good five inches across when full-blown. The center portion of the flower is spinel pink, verging on salmon, with a frame of rosy purple outer petals. The strong scent combines old rose and tea.

The choice of **Soeur Thérèse** (1931) is a curious one: it is an incorrigibly untidy plant with branching stems shooting off in all directions. The vase-shaped bud is Chinese yellow with jasper-red margins, quickly fading to a uniform light buffy yellow. Except for sharing its tremendous durability and vigor, 'Soeur Thérèse' seems to have contributed little to the match except to dilute 'Crimson Glory's' deep color and add a tiny chip of yellow to the base of each petal, an area so small that it is only visible when the flower begins to break up and fall. For those interested in heredity, 'Soeur Thérèse's' ancestors are of great historical importance as studs. One parent is the famous deep red Hybrid Perpetual 'Général Jacqueminot' which dates from 1852. A grandparent is the epoch-making 'Soleil d'Or,' the hybrid that captured the elusive genes of *Rosa foetida persiana* and made its unique characteristics available for the breeding of yellow roses.

**Mirandy** ('Night' x 'Charlotte Armstrong,' AARS 1945) resembles its famous parent in being fat, full and fragrant. It is somewhat closer to the purple end of the scale, with fuchsia inner petals in a nest of peony purple. 'Mirandy' hasn't quite the sturdy frame of 'Charlotte Armstrong'—some of its canes are a little thin—but it is still a wonderful piece of color, a perfect accessory for a Victorian Revival parlor.

**Rubaiyat** ('McGredy's Scarlet' x 'Mrs. Sam McGredy,' 1946) is the first rose to be recommended so far that is not descended from the patriarchs. The plant is tall with heavy canes. Foliage is ample, though badly crumpled by mildew in damp weather. The well-formed flowers are fuchsia purple with outer petals deepening to muted magenta. They carry a rich fragrance of old rose mingled with tea.

**Perfume Delight,** AARS 1974, has 'Peace' as one parent and a complex including 'Crimson Glory' on the other side. The tall buds, nicely incurved at the neckline, are intense fuchsia purple, paling as the flower ages to Persian rose with mauve edging. Buds are often produced in clusters: this calls for watchful disbudding. 'Perfume Delight' is a vigorous grower with profuse clean leaves, large and dull-finished, with an interesting olive cast. The name is overly flattering: the scent is neither constant nor pervasive, being absent in hot weather and sometimes replaced by a quite disagreeable sharpness. This is a rose for gardeners and flower arrangers who revel in the amaranth tones. It is hardly necessary to say that it should be kept away from orange-reds such as 'Tropicana.'

**Fragrant Cloud** (1968) has 'Peace' as one grandparent. It stands on the threshold between orange-red and rose-red. The inner surface of the high-centered bud is clear scarlet in dramatic contrast to the deep carmine exterior marked with a purple-black blaze towards the base. The flowers, which quickly lose their form as they open, are deep rose with a coral overlay, and end as a slightly grayed crimson. Multiple buds are the rule and should be thinned to produce one perfect bloom. 'Fragrant Cloud' is an immensely sturdy plant, one of the strongest growers in the BBG, with stout canes that spring outwards from the base. The leaves are large and dark green, with a varnishlike gloss that seems to repel fungus spores. The name overrates the fragrance, which is pungent rather than genuinely rose scented. At times it has a nose-prickling overtone that suggests the smell of turpentine—or more pleasantly, the tang of hot vinegar and spices that fills the house when homemade chili sauce or green tomato pickle is being cooked.

A discussion of orange-red roses must start with their source, **Independence** ('Crimson Glory' x 'Baby Chateau'). 'Independence' must have been viewed with astonishment and incredulity when it made its first incendiary appearance in 1943 in the fields of Wilhelm Kordes. The opening bud reveals petals of intensely saturated signal red in sharp contrast to the deep carmine exterior shadowed near the base with purple-black. It was an unprecedented color break, being the first rose to show a significant concentration of the

orange-red pigment pelargonidin. Some authorities consider the appearance of pelargonidin to be a mutation,
the spontaneous creation of a pigment hitherto unknown
in roses. This can hardly be the case, as one parent,
'Crimson Glory,' has exactly the same amount of pelargonidin as 'Independence'—measuring three on a scale
of 1 to 6. The other parent, 'Baby Chateau,' is a grandchild of 'Eva' which had earlier launched the revolutionary coral and shrimp pinks starting with 'Pinocchio'
and continuing with favorites such as 'Fashion,' 'Spartan' and 'Montezuma.' When the two pelargonidin-
bearing roses were crossed, the pigment became con-
centrated enough to overpower their crimson tones, at
least on the upper side of the petal where it is chiefly
located, while the underside retains its carmine base
color. This phenomenon is well described by Bertram
Parks in *The World of Roses* (New York: E. P. Dutton &
Co., 1962). In his description of 'Independence,' he
wrote: "This rose has had more influence on the colour
of modern roses than any other since 'Soleil d'Or.' Almost all the orange-scarlet and vermilion colouring, both
in Hybrid Teas and Floribundas, is derived from this
rose, and the evidence of it is nearly always shown by a
distinct purplish shade on the outside at the base of the
outer petals." This purple thumbprint is very conspicuous in 'Hallmark' and only slightly less so in 'Scarlet
Knight.'

'Independence' has a fault: its mature flowers fade to a
dismal magenta. If not disbudded, the aging central
flower—always the first to open—clashes with the newly
opening buds that encircle it. Nevertheless 'Independence' continues to be remarked for its extraordinary
depth of color, not yet approached by any of its dazzling

offspring. Visitors who want to pay their respects to this revolutionary flower will find a row of it near the north end of the third central bed counting from the pavilion, on the far side of 'Queen Elizabeth' with which it quarrels.

**Firelight,** introduced in 1971, has 'Crimson Glory' for one grandparent. The flower is large, full petaled and of exceptionally heavy substance. The upper surface is geranium red with an orange overlay; the underside is rich carmine. In intensity of color, it stands midway between 'Independence' and 'Tropicana'—not quite so saturated as the former but deeper and redder than 'Tropicana.' The bud is magnificently formed: it retains its tight spiral center as the broad guard petals slowly unfurl. The color holds without fading until petal drop. The plant is tall and heavy caned and looks vigorous despite susceptibility to mildew. It is unfortunate that 'Firelight' is so stingy with flower production. In the BBG, a row of five plants may show only two or at most three flowers. If it bloomed more freely, 'Firelight' would stand in the front rank of recent introductions.

**Tropicana** was bred in 1960 by Mathias Tantau, who is also credited with 'Fragrant Cloud.' 'Tropicana' has 'Peace' for one grandparent and was given the AARS award in 1963. 'Tropicana' can be described as a carmine rose overlaid with a translucent wash of orange. This casual observation has been endorsed in a study by three Dutch researchers, D. P. de Vries, H. A. van Keulen and J. W. de Bruyn, on the occurrence and distribution of various pigments in rose petals. By separating the layers of the petals of the rose 'Baccara,' de Bruyn found a predominance of pelargonidin in the upper layer and of

cyanidin in the lower. The flower is, then, in scientific
fact what it appears to the eye: carmine under a clear
orange glaze. To verify the coexistence of the two colors,
examine the underside of a petal from a mature bloom,
especially near the base where the carmine tone is so
pronounced that it verges on purple.

From a distance, 'Tropicana' glows with uncanny brilliance, a fiery intensity variously described as fluores-
cent or incandescent. 'Tropicana' is nudging 'Peace' as
the country's most favored rose and deservedly so, as its
dazzling tone illuminates any rose bed and retains its
clarity until the petals drop, not turning magenta as do
many orange-reds. The flowers are mid-sized, not huge
mops like 'Medallion' nor midgets like 'Pascali' but are
in good scale for garden display or to harmonize with
annuals in a mixed arrangement. The bud is high-
centered and, thanks to its 30 to 35 petals, keeps its excellent form as it slowly opens. 'Tropicana' has a moderate but pleasing scent, more fruity than flowery, recalling the winy tang of a cider mill or perhaps well-spiced
baked apples hot from the oven.

Admittedly, 'Tropicana' has faults. The plant is open
and irregular in form, often with awkwardly angled
canes, too few to make a luxuriant-looking bush. Foliage
is small, sparse and often marred by blackspot and mildew. Flowers are produced cyclically rather than
constantly—a wave of bloom, then none—which may be
an asset if your chief use for roses is as cut flowers. However deficient 'Tropicana' may be as a plant, there is no
question of the startling impact of its flowers. If you want
proof, carry a bunch on a city street. It is the only rose
I've ever known that makes approaching strangers stop
and ask, "Are those *real?*"

## Yellow Hybrid Teas

There may be a difference of opinion as to whether **Peace** is a bicolor or a yellow rose with pink ribbons. Since it tends to lose its pink borders entirely in cool weather, it seems justifiable to set it at the head of the list of yellow Hybrid Teas.

Though 'Peace' is listed as a Hybrid Tea, it is in fact far

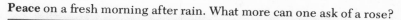

**Peace** on a fresh morning after rain. What more can one ask of a rose?

from typical of the class. Its stubby bud, full petalage and short neck, with leaves almost to its chin, are characteristic of the buxom old Hybrid Perpetuals, but the unrivaled delicacy of 'Peace's' coloring saves it from any hint of stodginess. The foliage is as dense and glossy as that of an English holly, an ornament in its own right and a superb setting for the luminous flowers. Their color varies with the temperature. In summer, the light mimosa-yellow petals are edged on the upper side with a translucent ribbon of grenadine pink, sometimes a narrow thread, sometimes a broad band of warm color. In late autumn, the pink is lacking and the rose is a rather undistinguished greenish yellow, hardly recognizable to those who know it only in its summer dress. The fragrance is also changeable: at times, the flower has a hint of old-rose scent; at others, no more than a fresh odor rather like the composite air of a greenhouse. The bud when one-third open is meltingly lovely. The petals have such heavy texture that they hold their shape without drooping so that the flower increases in beauty as it matures. 'Peace' was born in France in 1942 during World War II. The story of its perilous infancy is told on pages 231–232.

'Peace' is a happy exception to the general rule that roses with *Rosa foetida* blood—that is, all our modern yellow roses—are intolerant of heat and highly susceptible to blackspot and mildew. 'Peace' smiles at the worst a city summer can do in the way of punishing heat and humidity. While it isn't a prodigious summer bloomer, it produces enough flowers to pay its rent throughout the season. After more than thirty years, 'Peace' shows no sign of declining vigor and retains its proud rank as the world's favorite rose.

**Speaker Sam** (sport of 'Peace,' 1962) is a bolder version of 'Peace,' a masculine counterpart, taller, more emphatic in color, immensely vigorous but lacking the delicacy that wins 'Peace' its universal favor. 'Speaker Sam' has flowers of immense size and heavy substance but somewhat irregular form, with excessively reflexed petals and a crinkled texture that escapes coarseness but certainly lacks the refinement of finish so notable in 'Peace.' While these details may detract on close inspection, 'Speaker Sam' is a spectacular rose for garden effect, with all the merits of springing health and profuse bloom. Its *macho* image is somewhat tempered by a scent as innocent and artless as that of sweet clover.

Yellow roses are valued as harmonizers in the garden. They are eminently desirable for growing or cutting with the popular salmon-shrimp-flamingo varieties and are the only possible companions for hot oranges such as 'Firelight' and 'Tropicana.' It is a great misfortune that yellow roses tolerant of hot, humid climates can be counted on one hand. The lordly yellows bred in misty Ireland or the cool clean air of Oregon respond to the first suffocating day by going into shock and remaining comatose until autumn when they may recover enough to produce a few raddled blooms. In the majority of cases they dwindle and die.

Three yellow roses can be given qualified endorsement as reliable performers in trying climates. Two of them are oldsters: **King's Ransom** was introduced in 1961, **Lowell Thomas** in 1943. Neither traces its pedigree to the three patriarchal stud roses. The fact that they continue to be widely listed demonstrates their enduring worth and the fact that no better varieties have come along to supplant them. 'King's Ransom'—surely the most evocative name ever devised for a flower—is a tall, fairly robust plant with dark glossy foliage, remarkably

disease-resistant for a yellow rose. The buds are beautifully formed, of a light mimosa yellow deepening to canary. They keep their high spiral center until the flowers
are perhaps two-thirds open. At this point, their corset
strings snap: the flowers lose their trim waists and sag in
a loose blowzy way, with quilled and reflexed petals.
'Lowell Thomas' is a smaller plant than 'King's Ransom,'
with deeper yellow flowers produced dependably all
summer. Interestingly, in cool springs it shows a flush of
pinkish apricot in the center, a ghostly reminder of its
remote ancestor, 'Soleil d'Or.' 'Lowell Thomas's' buds
and partly opened flowers have acceptable form,
perhaps not so finely chiseled as those of 'King's Ransom,' but they end in the same disheveled mop of drooping petals.

The third yellow rose that survives unfavorable climates is **Summer Sunshine** ('Buccaneer' x 'Lemon Chif-
fon,' 1962). 'Summer Sunshine' belies its name: it is intolerant of midsummer heat and flowers only in spring
and fall. It is not a robust plant: its canes are thin, sometimes arching, sometimes too weak to support the flowers. The buds are intense chrome yellow with a narrow
blaze of jasper red. They retain their high center quite
well as they open, longer than do 'King's Ransom' and
'Lowell Thomas,' the only close rivals to 'Summer Sunshine' on the short roster of durable yellow roses. The
flower is mid-sized, measuring no more than 4¾ inches
when fully expanded. It matures to a lighter but still
arresting canary yellow, with the minor defect of not
being self-cleaning: withered flowers must be tidied
away. 'Summer Sunshine' flowers so generously in fall
that a few plants make a really compelling statement of
strong yellow, so eye-catching that they may not be
grudged their summer vacation.

Two other yellow roses may be included despite faults so serious that they would be crossed off the list if they were any other color. Yellow roses with sturdy constitutions and unflagging summer bloom are so rare that they demand mention even though their defects should be weighed before purchase.

**Lemon Spice** ('Helen Traubel' x seedling, 1966). If you are sated with strident colors, with heavy reds and with blazing oranges, the cool, delicate coloring of 'Lemon Spice' will bring welcome relief. It is the palest of yellows with a glow of light tangerine in the opening bud and in warm weather a faint border of shell pink. In cool weather, the pink disappears and the flower takes on a cool green tint, suggesting limeade instead of lemonade. Everything about the flower speaks of refinement and restraint. The bud, long and tapered, opens into a large flower with petals ample enough to make its maturity as lovely as the bud stage. The petals have a luminous quality that recalls the translucent beauty of its parent, 'Helen Traubel.' As you may recall, 'Helen Traubel' is a child of 'Charlotte Armstrong,' which is in turn a child of 'Soeur Thérèse,' the yellow bicolor with excessively long slender stems and erratic branching habit. Unfortunately, 'Lemon Spice' displays 'Helen Traubel's' inherited swan neck to an exaggerated degree. The flower is not specifically weak necked, as is 'Medallion,' but the stems are so long and limber that they arch over, tangling with other stalks and permitting the flowers to be torn by prickles when the wind sways them. The solution is to cut the flowers in bud. This would be no hardship as the flowers would show to best advantage against a dark background, while the curving lines of the stems would give an arrangement an airy grace quite lacking in the usual stiff-stemmed roses. It should be repeated in this qualified endorsement that 'Lemon Spice' is of little value for garden decoration but has great merit as a cut flower. Its scent? Hybrid Tea with lemon, to be sure.

**Eclipse** ('Joanna Hill' x 'Federico Casas,' 1935) is a slightly deeper yellow rose that performs admirably even in midsummer. It is noted for its beautiful bud— long, slender and flaring gracefully at the tip—though the mature flowers are skimpy and fleeting, without merit either in the garden or for cutting. The meager 25 petals are quick to open wide, then flop in a limp, dispirited way. Inexplicably, 'Eclipse' must have a train of admirers as it is still widely listed.

A book on roses is never finished: a last-minute discovery enables the discussion of yellow roses to end on a note of triumph. In October of 1978, a test rose, identified by the number under which the cross was recorded, opened some flowers of surpassing quality. The bud is light canary yellow, clear and luminous, with deeper tones in the depths of the slowly unfurling petals. The flower is full-petaled with a finish as smooth as a kid glove. The high conical center lasts for days even when the outer petals are broadly expanded. The variety has two special qualities that are exceptional in yellow roses: the flowers are delightfully fragrant and the plant is heavy-caned and apparently disease free, as it is clothed with unblemished leaves to the ground. As a measure of its sturdiness, a full-blown bloom weathered a driving rainstorm that left 'King's Ransom' and 'Summer Sunshine' sprawling on battered canes. The test rose, newly named 'New Day,' emerged unmarred and erect and sat for its portrait on the following day with the rain still on it. There's no telling as yet how the rose will

**New Day.**

perform in other regions, but gardeners in the New York area can rejoice in the production of a yellow rose that will thrive in our climate.

## YELLOW BLENDS AND BICOLORS

**Soleil d'Or** (1898), the seminal cross that merged *Rosa foetida persiana* with a Hybrid Perpetual, is the source of all our modern yellow roses as well as yellow blends and bicolors, that is, roses that are basically yellow but overlaid with various bands or washes of pink, orange or red tones. 'Talisman' (1929), 'President Herbert Hoover' (1930), and 'Condesa de Sastago' (1931) are early examples of the yellow-orange-red blends that will be remembered with affection.

'Soleil d'Or' flowers only once; it is so subject to mildew and blackspot that it is almost completely defoliated by fall; it smells of rotting orange peels. These are the evil traits bestowed by its *Rosa foetida* parent as the price of its inestimable gift of pure yellow. Despite its defects, 'Soleil d'Or' gives a fair account of itself, with a good showing of short-stemmed, fully double flowers set close together on arching canes. Petals are spoon-shaped, sometimes nested in neat radiating segments that suggest the quartered Tudor rose, sometimes in irregular masses. In the newly opened flower, the color is buffy amber with a strong suffusion of pinkish tangerine; it fades to light apricot on maturity. This may not be a variety you'd rush to add to your garden, unless you are a collector of historic roses, but it merits respectful attention for its expansion of the color range of modern roses. If you want to make the acquaintance of this epochal hybrid, there are two plants in the BBG located in the shrub border between the east walk and the trellised fence. You will find one plant in front of the climber 'Parade' on the fence and a second just north of the pillar rose 'Le Rêve.'

**Sutter's Gold** ('Charlotte Armstrong' x 'Signora,' 1954) has the lank neck and erratic multiple branching that 'Charlotte Armstrong' inherited from its parent 'Soeur Thérèse' and transmits to some but by no means all of its offspring. The buds and partly opened flowers of 'Sutter's Gold' are well formed and richly colored. The base color is cadmium orange bordered and suffused with strong coppery red, making a highly effective contrast as the outer petals unfurl. As it matures, the flower quickly grows limp and shapeless and fades first to light yellow with pink guard petals, then ends as a uniformly dull straw yellow. This is a variety for bud lovers or perhaps for exhibitors who select roses for their youthful perfection and are indifferent to the garden effect of the full-blown flowers.

**Yankee Doodle** ('Colour Wonder' x 'King's Ransom,' AARS 1976) is a superlatively vigorous plant with stout, almost thornless canes and shiny light green foliage that appears completely immune to fungus diseases. 'Yankee Doodle' is yellow shaded salmon and carmine. As to form, it looks as if an immensely full-petaled rose had had its upper two-thirds sawed off horizontally. What remains is a stubble of short petaloids surrounding a conspicuous and disfiguring mass of green carpels. It is a mystery that a grotesque flower such as 'Yankee Doodle' was thought worthy of introduction, and no less astonishing that it received the AARS award. It is hoped that the breeder will strive to preserve the strain's magnificent constitution while putting something that looks like a rose on top of it.

There are three roses—'Medallion,' 'Apricot Nectar' and 'Helen Traubel'—so similar in color that their mature flowers, cut and placed close together, can be distinguished only by size. They are described in catalogues as apricot, a term that does them less than justice. They are not unrelieved apricot-orange but come closer to cantaloupe with a light flush of coral pink. A treasured 1940 Bobbink & Atkins catalogue described an early tawny pink rose, 'Duquesa de Penaranda' (1931) as "cinnamon-peach," a far more accurate and appealing designation than mere apricot.

**Medallion** ('South Seas' x 'King's Ransom,' AARS 1973) is so large in scale that it should be placed with some consideration, perhaps at the back of a planting, as it overwhelms its companions if planted in a bed of

**Yankee Doodle.** An example of the freak flowers that diminish the worth of the variety.

average-sized HTs. 'Medallion' produces very tall canes, often insufficiently stiff to support the huge flowers which may measure more than six inches across. A row of 'Medallion,' with heads nodding in random directions, reminds one of a bench of sleepy passengers on a subway late at night. Even if moderately erect in dry weather, the blooms are certain to flop when weighted by rain so be sure to cut them for use in the house when a storm is predicted. As a child of 'King's Ransom,' 'Medallion' might be expected to have passable form. It starts out with a shapely bud, long-pointed and conical. The spiral center is retained for a scant one-third of the life of the flower which quickly loses its crispness and opens into a great fluff of petals, as airy as a swansdown powder puff. It is difficult to understand how judges overlooked the two defects of weak neck and loose form when they gave 'Medallion' the AARS award. Even if form is lacking, the color is luminous and appealing and, by its delicacy, dispels any suggestion of grossness that might be inferred from its size.

'Medallion' and 'Red Masterpiece' are depicted, or so the promotional material reads, on a United States postage stamp issued in June of 1978. The stamp is so small and the colors so pallid that the subject, let alone the identity of the roses, is hard to ascertain. A splendid opportunity was muffed. It is hoped that the postal authorities will not be discouraged by this fiasco but will instead issue another rose stamp comparable in size and artistry to the admirable environmental and wildlife series.

**Apricot Nectar** (seedling x 'Spartan,' AARS 1966) is a descendant of 'Eva' through 'Spartan' and may get its springing vitality from that patriarchal stud. 'Apricot Nectar' is a Hybrid Tea that thinks it's a Floribunda, or possibly the other way around. The studbook *Modern Roses* 7 (Harrisburg, Pa.: The McFarland Company, 1969) terms it a Floribunda but it is anything but typical: it grows a good six feet high and has flowers that measure five inches across. These are loosely double and are borne in clusters—that much at least conforms to Floribunda specifications—but because of the plant's soaring height, it looks more at home among Hybrid Teas and that's where we'll treat it. The plant has splendidly solid canes and thick foliage to the ground. The problem with 'Apricot Nectar' is that it produces one terminal bud which is speedily overtopped by side buds on shoots a foot or more long, so that the first flower is trapped at the bottom of a prickly cage and can be faintly seen as it struggles to open. There are two ways to deal with the trouble: you can disbud the cluster, sacrificing half-a-dozen potential blooms to get a large solitary flower, or you can remove the central bud, which will be maltreated anyway, and have sprays of smaller flowers on stems long enough for cutting and profuse enough for garden display. You might try both methods of coping with 'Apricot Nectar's' exuberance and see which way is better suited to your taste.

**Helen Traubel** ('Charlotte Armstrong' x 'Glowing Sunset,' 1951) doesn't look a day of its over-twenty-five years. It is much the same color as 'Medallion' though with more coral than cinnamon in some weathers. The buds are exceptionally long and graceful and are borne on tall slender stalks, not so rangy as 'Soeur Thérèse's' but still showing signs of kinship. The open flower is scant-petaled and somewhat flimsy in texture but, when viewed with the light behind it, it takes on a translucent seashell quality that has few rivals. The flowers are tea scented with sometimes a hint of true rose fragrance.

Unless given timely pruning, **Apricot Nectar** winds up in a cage.

The plant is apt to grow too tall and should be restrained by sharp pruning when flowers are cut. If possible, plant 'Helen Traubel' to the south or west of your seating area so that you can enjoy the singular beauty of its flowers when the light shines through them.

**Mojave** ('Charlotte Armstrong' x 'Signora,' 1954) has the same parents as 'Sutter's Gold' but the two have little else in common. 'Mojave' strongly resembles the older

'President Herbert Hoover' (1930), one of the early red-yellow blended bicolors. Each has only 25 petals, too few to make a substantial flower when fully open. However, the play of color on either side of the petals and at various stages of development is so intricate that it is impossible to convey adequately in words. Notes taken in the field read "outside of bud carmine and red-orange, opening deep yellow veined and flushed with flamingo pink" and a week later, "apricot petals flamed with rose madder to give a burnt orange overtone." Perhaps the best way to describe the diversity of color is to compare it to a sunset. The open flower reveals another fascination: in its center, a cluster of fat crimson stigmata, looking for all the world like the tube feet on the underside of a starfish, are bunched on a pale green field surrounded by a red ring. From the ring radiate dark red filaments tipped with tawny gold anthers, much in the style of 'Ivory Fashion.' To top off its attractions, 'Mojave' has a slight but appealing rose fragrance—surely a sufficient sum of merits to outweigh its deficiency of petals.

## SALMON AND PINK HYBRID TEAS

Add a little more pink to the basic yellow mix and you enter the range variously called salmon, coral, shrimp, flamingo, azalea or begonia pink. By the color chart, these are tints of vermilion, mandarin or poppy red, which are light reds on the orange side of scarlet. Due to the enthusiastic reception of these luminous colors, the complexion of the BBG rose garden has changed in the last thirty years from candy- and rose-pink to the livelier, more light-reflecting salmon pinks. While a few carmine-pink roses are still being bred, you'll find very few that are not relieved by yellow flares in the center or a wash of shrimp pink in the opening bud.

The revolution in pink roses and in the taste of their growers was set off by the introduction in 1940 of the Floribunda 'Pinocchio,' described as "pink suffused with golden salmon" in a 1957 Bobbink & Atkins catalogue. 'Pinocchio' still flourishes in the BBG and will be located for visitors when we come to deal with Floribundas. It is interesting and significant that one of 'Pinocchio's' parents was the Hybrid Musk 'Eva' which, in another line of breeding, resulted in the production of 'Independence' in 1943, the first large-flowered rose to show a preponderance of the dazzling orange-red pigment pelargonidin.

Some devotees of old roses deplore the shift to yellow-pinks which, as they rightly complain, clash with the mauves and carmine-pinks of the Damasks and Mosses. A judicious placement of old and new will keep the discord to a minimum. Like it or not, the public has joyfully embraced the salmon-pink roses and there's little doubt that they will dominate rose buying—and therefore rose breeding—in what we can see of the future.

**Pristine** ('First Prize' x 'White Masterpiece,' 1978) is as fresh and appealing as its name. It is the palest of shell pinks, slightly deeper on the outer petals and with a hint of light apricot-yellow in the depths. The blend of colors, so subtle and restrained, may be described as opalescent. The bud is beautifully formed with a high vase-shaped center that persists well into maturity. In its first year in the BBG, 'Pristine' didn't flower until late in the

**Pristine,** like all superior roses, is as beautiful when full-blown as on first opening.

season, and then sparingly, but its heavy canes and splendid maroon-shaded leaves promise outstanding performance when it is established.

**Gay Princess** ('Spartan' x 'The Farmer's Wife,' AARS 1967) traces its ancestry through 'Spartan' to 'Eva.' It is classed as a Floribunda but this is so absurd that it will be treated with the HTs where it belongs. It is a tall plant with flowers mostly produced singly or occasionally in small clusters which are easily disbudded. It is prodigally generous with bloom, not pausing even in midsummer dog days. The buds are superbly shaped in the ideal HT form, urn-shaped and flaring at the lip. Bud and open flower are pale dawn pink without the yellow illumination that makes 'Pristine' so warmly attractive. Lack of fragrance is the only serious demerit. 'Gay Princess' is one of the few roses that are set off to perfection in a silver container. If you have a mahogany or dark walnut console table, set a silver vase of 'Gay Princess' before the upturned leaf and you'll need no other reason

**Confidence.** The yellow flare in the throat is especially pronounced when the flower is backlit.

to include it in your planting. Visitors to the BBG, after discussing a nearby rose, are apt to say, "Now let me show you *my* favorite rose." Surprisingly often, it's 'Gay Princess,' as popular with men as with women. It is undoubtedly handicapped by its unfortunate name and is now seldom listed. If you can't locate a source, try 'Confidence' which lacks 'Gay Princess's' porcelain delicacy but adds a touch of yellow and the grace of intense fragrance.

**Confidence** ('Peace' x 'Michele Meilland,' 1951) is chunkier than 'Gay Princess,' as might be expected of a child of 'Peace,' and a little brighter and more varied in its coloring. Its bud is enlivened with a flush of shrimp pink which persists until the flower is fully open, when it matures to soft pink but keeps the yellow light in its heart. The plant is tall and vigorous with excellent clean foliage. 'Confidence' has an entrancing perfume, as rich and full-bodied as any Damask or Rugosa, pervasive enough to be enjoyed some yards away. The scent is delectable in summer and doubly so at the end of the season when it floats a breath of June on the cool autumn air.

**Seashell,** a grandchild of 'Tropicana,' received the AARS award in 1976. The color is delightful—a light-catching shrimp pink with flushes of gold. Buds are small, neatly formed but sparingly produced. The open flower is scant petaled, of rather thin substance, with a good tea scent. Canes are slender; foliage is overly subject to fungus disease, especially blackspot. The verdict on 'Seashell' is open. Certainly its clarity of color is a strong recommendation but the plant is not sufficiently robust to win unqualified approval.

**Sierra Dawn** ('Helen Traubel' x 'Manitou,' 1967) is as glowing as its name. Its coloring is much like that of

'Chicago Peace'—deep coral pink on a yellow-apricot base—but it is in every way a more refined flower. Whereas 'Chicago Peace' has leaves up to its chin, the flowers of 'Sierra Dawn' are carried on long clean stalks, a legacy through 'Helen Traubel' from 'Charlotte Armstrong.' The mature flower is light Persian rose with a yellow glow in the heart and on the underside of the petals. The plant is erect and sturdy with strong canes and dull-surfaced leaves with a maroon undertone. 'Sierra Dawn' adds to its visual attractions a piercingly sweet perfume, clear essence of rose without any additives such as fruit, wine or spice: it rivals the ancient 'Maiden's Blush' for purity of fragrance. Despite its outstanding merits as a garden rose, 'Sierra Dawn' has largely been dropped from catalogues. The BBG urges growers to make it available again and will gladly supply budwood for the purpose.

With **Tiffany** ('Charlotte Armstrong' x 'Girona,' AARS 1955) we move from shrimp-pinks into the range of rose-pinks with an undertone of yellow that gives them vibrancy. 'Tiffany' is one of the sturdiest, most disease-resistant plants in the BBG rose garden, with leafy, stiffly upright canes so tightly bunched that they suggest twigs bound into fagots for use as fuel. The color is deep rose-pink washed with salmon and enlivened with a gold flush at the base of the petals. The flowers are full enough to open slowly from their classic high-centered form. The most beguiling feature of 'Tiffany' is its deliciously pervasive old-rose scent, an extraordinary grace found in too few HTs and especially cherished when it is offered so freely.

**Chicago Peace** (1962) is a sport of its namesake, with 'Peace's' delicate coloring intensified to a blazing contrast. The flower is huge and full, showing a spiral center at first but opening quickly into a mass of ruffled petals, so firm in substance that they give the effect of a peony. The plant is of medium height and bears its enormous flowers on stems that are sometimes too short for good proportion. The center of the flowers is apricot-orange with the outer part of the petals broadly banded with strong Tyrian pink. Some visitors are entranced; one declared it his favorite rose; others consider it gaudy and prefer the tender coloring of the original 'Peace.'

**Spellbinder** ('South Seas' x unnamed seedling, 1975) was rated in 1977 as one of the loveliest of recent roses. At first glance, the flower appears as graduated shades of shell pink deepening to coral red. On close study, you find that the center has enlivening cream and yellow lights and that the light pink appears in irregular blotches, not just at the base of the petal but distributed at random over the darker areas, very much like the beautiful marbling of a variegated camellia. The resemblance is enhanced in the full-blown flower which opens quite flat, displaying its markings to great effect. The plant, as it grew in 1977, was tall with widely diverging canes which called for generous growing space. The leaves, dark green and thick textured, have a distinctive oddity: the terminal leaflet is often greatly enlarged and drawn out into a point somewhat in the manner of a mockernut hickory leaf. To our great surprise and disappointment, after its vigorous performance in its first years in the BBG, 'Spellbinder' began to decline in 1978. Towards the end of the season, the canes had died back so drastically that the plants were able to produce only one or two blooms. It is hoped that this is not a farewell appearance and that its reversal of health was due to some unusual combination of unfavorable clima-

Chicago Peace.

tic conditions and not to a suddenly revealed inherent
weakness.

**Duet** ('Fandango' x 'Roundelay') has 'Charlotte
Armstrong' as grandparent on both sides. It received the
1961 AARS award as a Hybrid Tea even though it is no
more than semidouble and its flowers are produced in
clusters. It is an unflagging performer, blooming without
pause even in steamy midsummer. Its wide-spreading
sprays of soft pink flowers have a fluttery effect much

**Duet** is one of the most prolific and latest-flowering roses in the BBG.

like the Floribunda 'Betty Prior' (1935) but are borne on taller and more rigid canes. 'Duet's' loosely formed flowers are soft rose-pink on the upper side—in some weathers, there is an enlivening hint of salmon—while the reverse is deep carmine pink. Since the petals are rippled, sometimes even twisted, the two shades are attractively displayed. The flower has a matt surface, ab-

**First Prize.**

sorbing light instead of reflecting it, so the mass effect is restful rather than brilliant. 'Duet' has a defect that bars it from a position where it will be observed at close range: the tawny-gold center of a newly opened flower quickly turns to dark brown, giving a suggestion of decay. 'Duet' is therefore best used at a distance, perhaps across a stretch of lawn where its clouds of ruffled flowers give it the look of a shrubby pink dogwood magically endowed with the property of blooming from early summer to killing frost.

**First Love** ('Charlotte Armstrong' x 'Showgirl,' 1951) is the first child of the buxom Charlotte to be rated as deficient in the number of its petals. The partly open flower is light rose-pink, veined and margined somewhat darker, with a small, hardly appreciable trace of yellow in the throat. The bud, slightly tinged with coral, is long and elegant, but the petals quill as fast as they unfurl, giving a spiky rather than a solidly rounded outline. The open flower is so thin in texture and so sparse petaled that it has no garden value.

**First Prize** ('Enchantment' seedling x 'Golden Masterpiece' seedling, AARS 1970) might have heard the criticism of 'First Love' and overreacted to it. The buds of 'First Prize' are rhodamine-pink, a tint of magenta, with deep rose-purple borders. They measure over 2¾ inches, as long as an index finger. As the petals peel away in sequence from this extraordinary length, they give the bud the outline of a pine cone. When one-third open, with the light-colored center still high and the dark-toned guard petals spread broadly around it, the effect is spectacular. The full-blown flower, because of heavy texture and a dearth of petals to fill the center, is somewhat coarse, but those who choose their roses primarily for size must expect to pay with loss of refinement. The plant has too few canes to make a well-filled bush but it is vigorous and disease resistant. The richly colored flowers look as if they should be fragrant. It is a mild disappointment to find them scentless.

**Friendship** ('Fragrant Cloud' x 'Miss All-American Beauty,' AARS 1979) is a tall bush with slender canes. It produced only three or four flowers in 1978. These were scant petaled, loose in form and thin in texture but with a pleasant fragrance. The color is spinel-red by the chart: rose-madder with a lot of neutral gray in it, or in more familiar terms, faded crimson leaning to magenta. The plant has a distinctive feature: its sepals are uncommonly long, some measuring over 2½ inches. They are elaborately slashed down the sides and sometimes ornamented with a spoon-shaped tip. As the sepals stand out stiffly horizontal, they make a flamboyant ruff below the base of the bud. However, decorative sepals are not sufficient reason to introduce a humdrum rose, let alone give it a highly publicized award.

**Eiffel Tower** (1963) has 'Charlotte Armstrong,' purveyor of excessively long stems, as one grandparent. The bud is exceptionally long and beautifully formed, with a tightly cinched waist and flaring lips. It opens mauve pink and fades to lilac. The trouble with 'Eiffel Tower' is that it tries to emulate its namesake in height. It is virtually impossible to keep within bounds: it produces budded shoots close below the current flower so that spent canes can't be drastically shortened without sacrificing the next wave of bloom. By the end of the season 'Eiffel Tower' is a cloud raker, so grotesquely lanky that it disrupts the uniformity of the moderate-growing roses in its neighborhood.

The buds of **Paradise** (not reported, AARS 1979) are not large but are admirably formed. Both the bud and the

partially open flower display a strong and somewhat dis-
quieting contrast: the base color is grayed lilac with
broad margins of intense cerise. The lilac quickly fades
out, leaving a flat, open-centered flower in two shades of
phlox pink. The plant has moderately strong canes with
quite good glossy foliage. Visitors have mixed feelings
about 'Paradise.' Some are enthusiastic; others say un-
easily, "Well, it's *different*. . . ." The flowers have a
faint tea scent with a teasing overtone which one visitor
said smelled like grass. He was out of range before anyone thought to ask whether he meant the lawn variety or
marijuana. Since 'Paradise' ends pink but starts out lilac,
it serves as a transition to out-and-out lavender roses.

## LAVENDER HYBRID TEAS

Lavender roses have something missing—quite liter-
ally. The lavender cast is not produced by adding
blue—something not yet possible, as the blue pigment
delphinidin has not appeared in roses—but by a frac-
tional diminution of cyanidin, the pigment chiefly responsible for the color of red roses. Lavender roses are
rather watery in appearance (though if you like them,
you may prefer to call the effect ethereal) and have little
garden value as they fade into atmospheric gray at a
slight distance.

**Sterling Silver** (seedling x 'Peace,' 1957). At the outset,
in discussing 'Peace's' role as a parent, it was stated
that—with one exception—'Peace' transmitted its splendidly sturdy constitution to its progeny. 'Sterling Silver'
is that exception: a puny plant that is likely to be taken
for a Floribunda if indeed it is noticed at all. The flower
has so little carrying power that it is virtually invisible

unless you are standing directly over it. Oddly enough, it continues to be listed. Perhaps the name promises something of value.

**Song of Paris** (1964) has 'Crimson Glory' as one grandparent. It has enough visual impact to rate a second look. The bud is well formed and keeps its spiral center for a long time. Foliage is clean and canes stout and vigorous though somewhat short. The flowers are so full that they sometimes ball in wet weather, and are not always self-cleaning. The color is a fairly saturated amethyst violet with buds a little more reddish. Buds are produced in large clusters and must be constantly and conscientiously disbudded to avoid muddles of malformed flowers. In the BBG, 'Song of Paris' is planted next to 'King's Ransom,' a much taller clear yellow. The alliance is mutually flattering and might well be copied in a home garden. 'Song of Paris' has an intriguing scent which various visitors, after sniffing diligently, concluded was that of artificially flavored sarsaparilla . . . or is it root beer?

**Heirloom** (two unnamed seedlings, 1972) varies in color with the weather. It is sometimes quite uniform reddish violet; at other times the petals, especially the inner ones, are bluish gray with a heavy veining of red-purple and with magenta borders. The flowers are so immensely full that they resemble Hybrid Perpetuals or cabbage roses. They are often too heavy for their stalks even when borne singly. As they tend to appear in large congested clusters, they need rigorous and vigilant disbudding. Canes are tall and weak; foliage is subject to fungus diseases and is apt to be greatly thinned by autumn.

**Lady X** (seedling x 'Simone,' 1966) is a tall, vigorous bush with well-branched erect canes. The flower is of excellent form, long in the bud and with a refined slender waist. The color is very dilute, hardly more than a wash of mauve on a gray-white ground. The stem is long with small leaves set at wide intervals, giving inadequate visual support to the flower. The most interesting aspect of the variety is the speculation that it might have been named for Madame X, Sargent's title for his scandal-rousing portrait of a haughty woman whose plunging black velvet gown reveals an expanse of flesh conspicuously tinted with lavender face powder. Unlike her putative namesake, who seems about to slip out of her clothes, 'Lady X' keeps her faded petals huddled tightly around her in a withered, discolored ball which must be removed for the sake of neatness.

## WHITE HYBRID TEAS

It is just a step from pale lavenders to white roses. There are few on dealers' lists, a statistic that no doubt reflects a lack of enthusiasm on the part of gardeners.

**White Masterpiece** (two unnamed seedlings, 1969) is superlative in form, of large size and heavy substance, with a cool greenish cast in its depths. If you plan to enter a white rose in a June flower show, you could make no better choice. However, the plant goes into shock with the first crushingly hot humid day. By autumn it is mostly defoliated and too seriously weakened to produce acceptable blooms, if indeed it recovers enough to try.

**Pascali** ('Queen Elizabeth' x 'White Butterfly,' AARS 1969) is the next best choice in white HTs. The flowers are of classic form, with a high urn-shaped center, slow

White Masterpiece.

spiral unfolding above a broad frame of guard petals, and a pleasant hint of yellow to warm its throat. However, it is distressingly small—too small, certainly, to be in accord with its tall-growing, narrow bush. Its parent 'Queen Elizabeth' may account for the disproportionate height of the canes in comparison with the size of the flower. The disparity is of course only evident in the garden and doesn't affect 'Pascali's' great merit as a cut flower.

**Frau Karl Druschki** (1901) presents a puzzle. It is classed as a Hybrid Perpetual and therefore might be supposed to belong in a discussion of shrub roses. One of its parents, 'Merveille de Lyon' (1882), is a Hybrid Perpetual; the other, 'Mme. Caroline Testout' (1890), is an early Hybrid Tea. This mixed lineage seems to give it

**Pascali.**

place in either camp. In any case, the Frau is far from typical of HPs in general. Most of these bloom only once and are strongly perfumed, whereas the Frau flowers freely all season and is almost scentless. One of the quiet pleasures of spending time in the BBG rose garden is the opportunity to enlist responsive visitors in an effort to put a name to a fragrance. One guess for the Frau was whipped cream; another, a lightly scented toilet soap, sometimes specified as Camay.

'Frau Karl Druschki' is the only HP listed in the catalogues of general rose growers, that is, not exclusive specialists in old roses. From this we can deduce that it harmonizes with HTs in a rose bed—and indeed it has a certain formality that makes it look ill at ease in the often rampant company of a shrub rose border. In the New York Botanical Garden, the Frau forms a six-foot column studded with great white flowers, so regular and symmetrical that you may have to touch it to convince yourself that it is a living plant and not a plastic construction designed to decorate a bank lobby. In the BBG, the Frau would pass for an extra-robust HT, tall and well filled, with strong canes to support its buxom flowers. These are of a curiously lifeless pure white and have for some visitors a rather funereal air, looking as if they might be carved in marble to ornament a Victorian tombstone. The flower is so full that it sometimes balls in hot rainy weather. However, if you want an iron-hardy, disease-free white rose, 'Frau Karl Druschki' has been filling the bill for seventy-seven years and shows no sign of losing its youthful vigor.

# 5

# Floribundas

Floribundas are a volatile tribe. Great numbers are launched every year with elaborate fanfare but without adequate testing or critical selection. Most of them vanish without trace, both from catalogues and from the gardens of disgruntled buyers. This dumping of unproved varieties on the market seems shortsighted in the extreme, as gardeners who have watched their highly touted roses dwindle and die will be wary of believing catalogue claims in future and, very likely, of buying from the firm that misrepresented its offerings.

Floribundas are primarily landscape subjects to be used somewhat like azaleas. They should be massed in groups of six or more of a single variety in order to produce a unified statement of color. At close to $5.00 a plant, a mistake multiplied by six can mean a substantial loss. For this reason, it is of prime importance to select sturdy, free-flowering, enduring varieties. The following assessments have been made after prolonged and intensive study of the more than 900 varieties grown in the

BBG. Conditions are ideal for testing as all the roses share the same exposure, soil, light, spraying and fertilization. If one rose grows and flowers exuberantly while its neighbor mopes and sickens, the difference must rest with the variety and not the growing circumstances. The authors believe that gardeners will prefer to be warned of a plant's defects in print, rather than discovering them after purchase in their gardens, even if the critical process entails a distasteful number of negative judgments. It should be stressed that these reports are based on performance in the BBG and do not necessarily apply to roses grown in other climates, especially those with cooler and less humid summers.

Some students of roses are fascinated by heredity and the unforeseeable surprises that make rose breeding a breathless adventure. These readers may welcome a capsule outline of the ancestry of our best Floribundas. Plain gardeners who are impatient to get on to descriptions and assessments of roses can skip this historical background without loss.

**Eva,** that mysterious Hybrid Musk, by all means heads the list. It is not grown at present in the BBG but we have some tentative leads and hope to secure a plant. In all likelihood, it would be trained to one of the vacant pillars on the west border of the garden. If you recall, 'Eva' was the seminal rose whose grandchild, 'Baby Chateau,' when mated with 'Crimson Glory,' produced 'Independence,' the first large-flowered orange-over-carmine rose. 'Eva's' blood is so prepotent that its influence is apparent in its offspring through six or eight generations. Despite an excursion into the large-flowered roses with 'Independence,' most of 'Eva's' progeny are Floribundas. Chief among them is 'Pinocchio,' the ut-

Pinocchio.

terly delightful soft pink-and-apricot blend that first brought the salmon tones into garden roses. 'Eva's' grandchild 'Baby Chateau,' a dark red semidouble, isn't much to look at but it appears again and again in the bloodlines of favorite roses. 'Floradora' in turn is an improbable cross between 'Baby Chateau' and the

Chestnut Rose, *Rosa roxburghii,* which has single pink flowers, ferny pinnate leaves with fifteen narrow leaflets and large elliptical fruits armed with sharp spines like a sea urchin's. Mathias Tantau must have been in a sportive frame of mind, an I'll-try-anything-once mood, when he devised this farfetched mating. Nevertheless, as often happens when a species rose brings vigorous new genes into the often inbred garden rose bloodlines, the result had a powerful influence. 'Floradora,' while not an outstanding rose by today's standards, figures in the breeding of 'Queen Elizabeth,' 'Montezuma,' 'Duet,' and even more recently, 'First Edition,' AARS winner for 1977. Finally, 'Fashion' repeats the original mating by uniting the patriarch 'Crimson Glory' with 'Eva's' child 'Pinocchio.' These names—'Pinocchio,' 'Baby Chateau,' 'Floradora' and 'Fashion'—wind through the pedigrees of Floribundas like a colorful ribbon of honor. There is scarcely a worthy variety that doesn't display, however remotely, 'Eva's' coat of arms.

## SALMON AND PINK FLORIBUNDAS

**Pinocchio** ('Eva' x 'Golden Rapture,' 1940) takes pride of place in a discussion of Floribundas because of its historic importance. Don't imagine, however, that it is a faded relic of antiquity. Far from it! It's a charmer—fresh faced, smoothly finished and delectably colored. The clusters are compact nosegays with flowers on one level on stems over six inches long, enough to permit cutting for corsages or small arrangements. The beautifully formed buds open to show a peach-pink interior framed in coral outer petals with an enlivening glow of yellow in the throat. The yellow is especially noticeable when the half-open bud is seen with the sun behind it. For an added fillip, the outer end of each petal dips and then rises to a tiny point that recalls the mucro tipping the perianth segments of the loveliest daffodils or, on a larger scale, the linked ogee curves that meet in a spire on the dome of the Taj Mahal. The mature flower, which may measure three inches across, pales to light rose-pink, in harmony with the younger buds. Canes are sturdy and upright; foliage is clean and ample. The flowers, produced without pause throughout the season, have a light, fresh, somewhat fruity scent, pleasing to humans and especially attractive to honeybees which add greatly to a photograph if you can catch them in action. You'll want to pay your respects to this prestigious flower which combines with grace its role of horticultural landmark with the secret of eternal youth. Look for it in the first bed in the center row in the main garden, about three-quarters of the way to the far end as you stand with your back to the latticed pavilion.

In **Fashion** ('Pinocchio' x 'Crimson Glory,' AARS 1950), 'Pinocchio's' hint of salmon is intensified and established as a positive force in modern rose breeding. It is a clear shrimp pink with golden lights in the depths. It was described by Bertram Parks in *The World of Roses* as "The first variety ever to be raised of this particularly charming colour." 'Fashion' is more than a milestone in rose breeding: it is a healthy, durable, free-blooming Floribunda well worth growing for garden decoration and sparkling cut flowers. The neatly designed blooms are harmonious in combination with 'Apricot Nectar' and 'Helen Traubel.' Placed in front of either of these varieties, 'Fashion' would counteract any tendency to leggi-

Fabergé.

ness in the taller plants. Visitors to the BBG can verify that 'Fashion' retains its luminous appeal: it fills the terrace beds south of the pavilion.

**Ma Perkins** ('Red Radiance' x 'Fashion,' AARS 1953) is somewhat pinker than 'Fashion,' that is, nearer coral than shrimp but with the same yellow glow in the heart and suffusing the pink undertone. It is not so free flowering as 'Fashion' though the flowers, when produced, are much larger—up to 3½ inches. It is a match for 'Fashion' in sturdy constitution and disease-resistant foliage and has in addition a delightful fragrance, an infrequent but welcome asset in Floribundas.

**Fabergé** (seedling x 'Zorina,' 1969) has two measures of 'Pinocchio' blood through 'Zorina' whose parents are a 'Pinocchio' seedling and 'Spartan.' It is an enchanting flower of perfect form and luscious color, hovering in the delectable range between shrimp and shell pink with an animating yellow light towards the base. Its form rivals that of 'Pascali'—high praise indeed—with a tightly cinched waist, flaring lips and infinitely slow spiral unfolding, with an eventual spread of over four inches. The outer petals quill more than could be wished, but their fullness (48 to 54 petals, an extraordinary number for a Floribunda) keeps the flower from looking skimpy. 'Fabergé' retains its high-centered form for days in water, making it one of the few Floribundas that is as valuable as a cut flower as for garden decoration. Most of the shoots produce single flowers; a few have one or two side buds which can easily be removed. In midsummer the buds sometimes come in clusters. The center flower is short stemmed but the encircling blooms have 5- to 8-inch stems, quite long enough for small arrangements. In the garden, 'Fabergé' is best placed by itself as its porcelain delicacy would be overpowered by larger roses in a mixed planting.

'Fabergé' is the very antithesis of the blatant orange roses that make their claim fifty feet away and don't improve on closer inspection. Like the works of the master jeweler whose name it bears, 'Fabergé' is a subject for quiet contemplation and intimate enjoyment on your study table or under the lamp beside your reading chair. It is beguiling by itself or in combination with fine-textured, gentle-toned flowers such as pale yellow snapdragons, blue lace flower, violet scabiosa or light blue delphiniums. If further inducement is needed, 'Fabergé' has a delicate, volatile scent which makes guests exclaim with pleasure when a vase is set between them and an open window.

For some reason, the studbook *Modern Roses 7* classifies 'Fabergé' as "For greenhouse use." As a fact, it is as hardy as the average rose in the BBG: it came through the last two cruelly punishing winters without protection and with no frost damage. One caution, though, since we are not gardening in Paradise: though the plant is highly resistant to disease, it can be attacked by mildew in prolonged wet weather, especially on the vulnerable bud stalks. Since it would be a pity to lose a single flower, be sure to apply a fungicidal spray before the onset of a predicted spell of rain.

In Floribundas, the balance between candy pink and salmon or shrimp is just about even. If Grandifloras are added, the scale tips slightly towards the candy side.

**Gene Boerner** ('Ginger' x ['Ma Perkins' x 'Garnette Supreme'], AARS 1969) is classed as a Floribunda. Its near twin, **Queen Elizabeth** ('Charlotte Armstrong' x 'Floradora,' AARS 1955) is listed as a Grandiflora, at least in this country where the class was invented. Both are tall, vigorous and disease resistant. Flowers are rose-pink of pleasing clarity and with a slight tea scent. If a choice is to be made, since you wouldn't want two such similar plants, 'Queen Elizabeth' easily gets the nod. It is an unflagging summer bloomer and keeps its unblemished complexion until the petals drop, whereas 'Gene Boerner' develops unsightly blotches and streaks of magenta, the vegetable equivalent of a bad case of acne. 'Queen Elizabeth' is especially attractive in autumn when its cupped flowers, filled with a mass of shorter petals in the manner of a Bourbon, take on a translucent quality, giving them an air of delicacy they lack in midsummer.

Better still, select **Pink Parfait** ('First Love' x 'Pinocchio,' AARS 1961). Listed as a Grandiflora, it has a more compact form than most of its leggy class, a neatness of habit which it must inherit from 'Pinocchio' since 'First Love' tends to be lanky. 'Pink Parfait' is one of the best looking plants in the BBG, vigorous and clean foliaged,

**Pink Parfait.**

seldom if ever out of bloom and keeping up a brave display until killing frost. The mid-sized flowers repeat 'Pinocchio's' coloring in Hybrid Tea form; rose-pink outer petals, margined with deeper rose, framing a long-lasting spiral center of coral pink with a hint of yellow at the base. The outer petals quill with age but this is not pronounced enough to detract from the flowers' charm. There is a slight musky scent, not roselike but quite pleasing. Unlike 'Queen Elizabeth' and 'Gene Boerner,' which carry their flowers at the top of tall leafy canes, 'Pink Parfait' distributes its flowers along the short outer canes as well so that the entire bush, not just its top story, is covered with bloom. In 'Pink Parfait,' the size of the flowers and the height of the canes are in better proportion than is the case with most Grandifloras. If the class is to be continued, it is hoped that the trend towards lower and bushier plants will be maintained—in which case we'll have some excellent large-flowered Floribundas. However, some discretion must be used in making sure that large flowers are provided with stems long enough so that they can open without interference from their neighbors in the same cluster.

**Bon Bon** ('Bridal Pink' x seedling, AARS 1974) is an example of the distressing muddle that occurs when HT-sized flowers are carried in tight, short-stemmed clusters that would be in good proportion for a one-inch Polyantha. 'Bon Bon' is a vigorous bush with a curious flat-topped, spreading habit. If you cut a flower free from the mass and shake it gently to coax it to expand, it proves to measure a good five inches. A flower of this span, jammed into a narrow cranny between adjacent buds, is of course unable to open but remains folded double like a frankfurter roll. The flowers are either not self-cleaning or the mass is too tightly compressed to permit petals to fall. The result is a most unpleasant aggregate of buds, pinched flowers and dead petals. The flower, when it has room to open, is a lovely color: radiant coral-rose with a silvery reverse. If the AARS award beguiled you into buying 'Bon Bon,' it may be possible to minimize its faults by drastic disbudding. You could try reducing the buds to three widely spaced ones on the outermost edges of the cluster. For another approach, patterned on time-release cold capsules, you could retain three or four buds of different stages of development in the hope that the most mature would finish blooming before the next in line needed its space.

**Pink Bountiful** ('Juanita' x 'Mrs. R. M. Finch,' 1945) has a Floribunda for one parent but, unlike 'Pink Parfait,' not one with the cherished blood of 'Eva.' The flowers are in two shades of rose-pink, slightly deeper on the underside in the manner of 'Duet.' They lack the yellow throat and the contrasting colors that make 'Pink Parfait' so glowing. Plants are not strong and, because of susceptibility to fungus diseases, grow bare-shanked towards the end of the season.

As long as we're admitting Grandifloras to a chapter on Floribundas, we may as well stretch the category to include two Polyanthas, the forebears of Floribundas. The two, 'The Fairy' and 'Cécile Brunner,' are still frequently listed, having kept their place by sheer merit. **The Fairy** (1941) is no more than a foot high, spreading to the ground, with absolutely disease-proof, light green *Rosa wichuraiana* foliage inherited from its grandparent 'Dorothy Perkins.' The small flowers, borne in tight clusters, are light rose-pink fading to white in hot sun. The petals are crinkled and have the pinked edges often found in Ramblers. 'The Fairy' is never out of bloom. As the plants keep their compact form with little or no prun-

**The Fairy.**

ing, they are ideal for low borders or to edge paths—with
the added advantage that their dense prickly canes discourage short cuts without being unpleasantly aggres-
sive about it.

**Cécile Brunner** was bred in 1880. Its parentage is
hazy: *Modern Roses 7* gives it as "probably a Polyantha x
'Mme. de Tartas,' " a Tea Rose dating to 1859. Graham
Stuart Thomas, in his invaluable *The Old Shrub Roses*
(London: Phoenix House Ltd., 1955), gives further
background on the origin of Polyanthas, a complex
pedigree whose characteristics are combined in 'Cécile
Brunner.' The first Polyanthas were developed by cross-
ing the Japanese *Rosa multiflora* with 'the Dwarf Pink
China, raised in England in 1805, where it was known as

*R. Lawranceana.* The plate of this variety in Curtis's *Botanical Magazine* for 1815 shows a delicate blush pink five-petaled rose with hair-thin branching stems and small leaves. The text, printed with the long *s* which we can only approximate with an *f,* states that "Our prefent fubject is the moft dwarfifh Rofe that has ever fallen under our notice." The introduction of *R. multiflora* blood contributed stamina and light green, slightly glossy foliage unaffected by fungus diseases. The infusion of Tea Rose added more petals and some fragrance, but the wiry stems that support the airy sprays of flowers are pure China.

**Cécile Brunner.** The upper left flower shows a button eye, a feature that adds a subtle finish to old roses.

'Cécile Brunner' is affectionately known as The Sweetheart Rose. Its high-centered buds are ⅝ inch tall. On first opening, their color is fresh peach pink with sometimes a suffusion of apricot. As they mature, the flowers pale to light shell pink and may measure all of 1½ inches across. The inner petals are slender, almost daisylike, a resemblance enhanced by the perfect button eyes that suggest a daisy's central disk. 'Cécile Brunner' might win a contest for the most roses produced during the season—in numbers, that is, though not in bulk. Well past the middle of October, it still sends up its large sprays of buds, thirty or more on a single cane, and evidently has no intention of winding down until snow flies.

'Cécile Brunner' has a light and teasing fragrance: a base of tea, a trace of rose and a hint of almonds and honey. Marzipan? Macaroons? Nougat? If you don't mind getting your knees grass stained, you can test your acuity by trying to put a name to the scent. 'Cécile Brunner' is planted in north-south rows along the east side of the first and second beds in the center row. Since 'Cécile Brunner' is approaching its hundredth birthday, still looking younger than springtime, it deserves an extra tribute of appreciation.

**First Edition** (AARS 1977) has 'Floradora' as one grandparent. The flowers are charmingly formed, with a high but open center and broad guard petals. The color is basically deep rose with just enough suffusion of coral to give it sparkle. Both in form and color, the flowers bear an uncanny resemblance to those of the low-growing *indicum* azalea, *Rhododendron balsaminaeflorum*. It is regrettable that 'First Edition's' trace of 'Eva's' blood, filtered down through 'Floradora,' is not enough to endow the variety with stamina. The plants are less than a foot tall and seem to be shrinking. It is unlikely that they will be alive another year.

**Montezuma** ('Fandango' x 'Floradora,' 1955) has distinguished ancestry. 'Fandango' is a child of 'Charlotte Armstrong,' that redoubtable matron; 'Floradora' is traced to 'Eva' through 'Baby Chateau.' 'Montezuma' is a credit to its forebears: classed as a Grandiflora, it is a prodigious producer of flowers of near-HT quality. The color is in the same vibrant range as 'Tropicana,' that is, a carmine base with a transparent orange overlay. In 'Montezuma,' the carmine tone predominates, which makes it easier to group harmoniously with other roses. 'Montezuma' is a tall, erect rose whose handsome foliage clothes it to the ground. The flowers are borne in spreading clusters, all but the center one having stems long enough to use at the neckline of a mixed arrangement if not in an all-rose vase. As is usually the case with cluster roses, the center flower opens first and fades just as the surrounding buds are opening, often making a disagreeable contrast. 'Montezuma' is not a flagrant offender in this respect but still you may want to snip out the aging flower so it won't detract from the fresh new blooms. When the entire cluster is spent, cut the cane back quite sharply to keep the plant from growing too tall. The Floribunda 'Spartan' is a perfect color match for 'Montezuma' and, when set in front, conceals the flowerless base of the taller plant.

'Montezuma' puts the spice of variety into its flower patterns. Some buds unfurl in a normal spiral. In others, the outer petals open to form a flat collar while the center remains in a tight sphere. This is not a defect—not the ugly balling which afflicts some very full-petaled roses in wet weather—but a rather appealing oddity. Yet again, 'Montezuma' has the engaging trick of tilting its central

Spartan.

cone to one side while letting its outer petals flare out on the other. If 'Montezuma' were a shade less portly, the effect might remind one of a Spanish dancer with castinets held high and trailing skirt kicked to one side. 'Montezuma' adds to its merits an astonishing frost resistance: it may still put on a brave show of bloom after other roses are limp and blackened. Lack of fragrance is the only demerit to be marked against this outstanding rose.

**Spartan** ('Geranium Red' x 'Fashion,' AARS 1955) is in many ways a smaller edition of 'Montezuma' with much the same orange-over-carmine coloring. You won't find

"rosy vermilion" on any color chart, but if you can rec-
oncile these contradictory terms you will have a good
picture of 'Spartan.' The plant is taller than the average
Floribunda and quite erect, so that it makes an excellent
hedge. The bud and partly open flower are charmingly
formed and just the right size for a buttonhole or small
arrangement. They have a fault as they mature: the petals droop until they touch the stem, giving the fully open
flower the taller-than-wide outline of a thimble. If this
last stage offends a purist's eye, flowering is so profuse
that spent flowers can be snipped off without diminishing the display.

## ORANGE FLORIBUNDAS

Unlike the newer Hybrid Teas, which favor salmon
and shrimp tones, the recent Floribundas concentrate on
orange, some varieties softened with washes of pink or
tangerine, others flaunting the most uninhibited, often
garish displays of nasturtium, capsicum and fire red. The
obsession with orange is puzzling: it is too assertive to
combine harmoniously with other colors and is very seldom used as the dominant tone in interior decoration so
the flowers have no value for use indoors. It is perhaps
fortunate that few of the recent offerings are of top rank
so the list can be quickly pared to a manageable handful.

**Floradora,** AARS 1945, leads the list of orange-red
Floribundas solely on its historical value. As you may
recall, it is reputedly the product of an unlikely match
between 'Eva's' grandchild, 'Baby Chateau,' and the
Chinese wildling *Rosa roxburghii.* When first
mentioned, it was remarked that the breeder, Mathias
Tantau, must have been in a sportive mood when he

made the cross. On second thought, he may have been indulging in a recondite joke designed to mislead his competitors. If you want to examine *R. roxburghii* at the BBG, follow the west path nearly to its north end. After you pass under the last of the double arches, look for the rose 'Carmine Pillar' on your left. *R. roxburghii* is just beyond it. The bush has some very distinctive characteristics: pinnate foliage with seven pairs of narrow leaflets and a terminal one; bark that peels in papery shreds, exposing a pale gray trunk; and prickles often paired oppositely, not hooked but shaped like a bracket or, more precisely, a console, that is, flat on top and curving beneath to the stem. By all rights, 'Floradora' should have inherited some of these traits and so should her descendants 'Queen Elizabeth,' 'Montezuma' and 'Duet.' This is simply not the case. 'Floradora's' leaflets are conventionally rounded and often are in threes or at most five to a leaf. The three progeny have strongly hooked prickles and notably broad leaflets. If the attributed breeding was a joke on Tantau's part, whatever he used resulted in a second generation of superlative roses. As to 'Floradora,' you can find it in the second central bed, two rows from the south end. It is a rather weak, slender-stemmed plant, very shy flowering. When you can find a bud, it is of a brilliant fire orange fading to spinel red—the flowers not large, rather fleeting, but carrying the priceless 'Eva' inheritance which it transmits to its offspring.

'Duet' and 'Montezuma' are among the five most flowery and latest-blooming roses in the BBG, with 'Queen Elizabeth' a close runner-up. This may be coincidence, but any coincidence that chalks up three record holders among nine-hundred-odd contenders is worth a second

look. It might be productive of more such happy coinci-
dences if 'Floradora' can be brought back into the breeding pool.

The speculation as to 'Floradora's' parentage is of
course based on external evidence. More sophisticated
techniques such as a chromosome count would be
needed for certain determination. Meanwhile, to sum up
the findings of amateur detection, it's a wise rose that
knows its own father.

**Cathedral** (['Little Darling' x 'Goldilocks'] x 'Irish
Mist,' AARS 1976) has a share of 'Eva's' blood through
'Little Darling' whose parents are 'Baby Chateau' and
'Fashion.' Nevertheless, based on its sorry performance
during the summer months, it was placed on the list of
failures. It rallied with the first cool weather to put on a
most attractive show of semidouble flowers of rather
flimsy texture and variable color: some are muted orange
with gold at the base of the petals, others are a more
saturated orient red. 'Cathedral' has an oddly unroselike
look. With its large ruffled flowers set down among the
foliage, it resembles the dwarf azalea 'Pink Gumpo' in
profusion of bloom and placement of flowers but of
course not in color. Some of the flowers fade quite pret-
tily to white at the base while retaining their orange or
red outer margin. The coloring and rippled tissue-paper
texture make them look more like Shirley poppies than
roses. Clearly 'Cathedral' is a plant for cool climates. As
to its future in the BBG, we will have to see whether the
growth it puts out in spring and fall can compensate for
summer dieback.

**Irish Mist** ('Orangeade' x 'Mischief,' 1966) has a double helping of 'Eva's' blood: on the one hand through
'Orangeade,' a child of 'Independence,' and on the other
through 'Mischief' which has 'Peace' and 'Spartan' as

parents. Like 'Cathedral,' it did so poorly in summer that it was crossed off the recommended list. With the advent of cool nights, it sent up tall, strong canes and a good show of full-petaled four-inch flowers. The nicely formed buds are light vermilion and fade to 'Tropicana' color when mature. 'Irish Mist' would doubtless be a splendid variety for more northerly areas, but those who want roses all summer would do better with a heat-tolerant plant like 'Contempo.'

**Contempo** ('Spartan' x ['Goldilocks' x ('Fandango' x 'Pinocchio')], 1971) has a formidable register of famous ancestors to which it brings added luster. 'Spartan' and 'Pinocchio' trace back to 'Eva,' while 'Fandango' is a child of 'Charlotte Armstrong.' 'Contempo' is a nonstop bloomer, unaffected by midsummer heat and humidity. In hot weather the flowers are deep yellow underneath and nasturtium orange above—not a glaring orange but subtly softened with pink until it approaches shrimp red. With the coming of cool autumn weather, the pink cast intensifies and the reverse of the petals turns from yellow to peach with warming flushes of carmine. As an added fillip for acute observers, the center of the open flower shows deep crimson stigmata with wheat-colored tips, a pleasing contrast to the gold zone at the base of the petals. A full-blown flower may measure 4½ inches across and, with its thirty or more petals, would pass for a Hybrid Tea. The habit of the plant is tall and twiggy, somewhat open in effect because of its small leaves, but these make up for lack of density by their high gloss and apparent immunity to disease. The flower has a spherical center, not the ideal urn shape, but it nevertheless opens so slowly that the contrast between the upper and lower sides of the petals is evident for a long period. With really cold weather, the flowers lose their bicolor effect and turn a less attractive uniform burnt orange.

'Contempo' tends to develop overlong, thin flowering shoots at the end of the season. As in the case of 'Apricot Nectar,' these shoots trap the central flower and prevent its opening. It might be possible to control this spindly tendency by cutting off spent canes rather severely towards the end of August. 'Contempo' has another fault: its faded flowers hang on, browned and unsightly, and by their numbers, present a chore for the gardener with a passion for neatness. In the final tally, 'Contempo' has such outstanding merits that they far outweigh its undisciplined behavior in October.

With **City of Belfast** ('Evelyn Fison' x ['Circus' x 'Korona'], 1968) we cross into the fighting orange band of the spectrum. 'City of Belfast' dips into the 'Eva' bloodstream through its grandparent 'Circus' but doesn't share 'Circus's' harmonious coloring or sturdy vitality. It is a low-branching plant of moderate growth with clean foliage. The buds are charmingly formed with a tight center framed in ruffled petals. The open flower, about 2½ inches across, is loose in form and lacks fullness. The color varies with the temperature from fire orange to signal red, a saturated scarlet, sometimes a uniform color, sometimes lighted with a deep gold zone at the base of the petals.

**Fire King** ('Moulin Rouge' x 'Fashion,' AARS 1960) is almost exactly the same blazing color as 'City of Belfast' but its brilliance is dulled by black shadowed patches on the tips of the petals, especially noticeable in the bud and partly open flower when the margins appear to be charred. 'Fire King' is much taller than 'City of Belfast,' with canes that tend to arch under the weight of their congested flower clusters. It is excessively subject to mildew and may be bare in the shanks by late summer.

**Matador** ('Konigen der Rosen' x 'Zorina,' 1976) is even more dazzling than 'City of Belfast' and 'Fire King.' Its mid-sized flowers are of flame red shading to golden yellow at the base. Texture is admirably firm: the outer petals, crimped and scalloped at the ends, flare crisply above a neatly indented waist. The compact plant is densely furnished with dark leaves with a bronze cast and metallic sheen. The flowers are closely set against this mirror-finish background with incandescent effect. Because of its tight-packed leaves and short flowering stems, 'Matador' makes an outstanding intermediate-sized tree rose. This may be the ideal use for it: separated from competing plants and held well above the damp soil, it may escape the mildew that afflicts it when grown in a crowded bed. Its parent 'Zorina' is a cross between a 'Pinocchio' seedling and 'Spartan.' 'Zorina' was introduced in 1963 and quickly disappeared from catalogues. It appears to be a sleeper that has little effectiveness in the garden yet is of value as a parent. It turns up in several recent crosses in addition to 'Matador,' chiefly in the delectable 'Fabergé' and less successfully in 'Charisma.'

Mention of 'Charisma' is a reminder that we might as well get the adverse judgments done with. 'Charisma' and 'Bahia' trace their faults to a common parent, **Rumba** ('Masquerade' x ['Poulsen's Bedder' x 'Floradora'], 1962). 'Rumba' is a stiff little flower with stubby, tightly imbricated petals of strong yellow bordered with red-orange. Flowers are short necked and on first opening, as flat as a dime and not much larger. With age, the petals recurve so sharply that they touch the stem, ending by looking more like a French marigold than a rose. The maturing flower goes through inharmonious color changes, first darkening to Turkey red, then fading to gray with carmine-pink edges. Spent flowers end as speckled cobweb gray and hang on the plant instead of dropping cleanly. The plant has thin canes and is much afflicted with blackspot.

**Charisma** ('Gemini' x 'Zorina,' AARS 1978) is a grandchild of 'Rumba' through 'Gemini.' It is a better plant than 'Rumba,' with sturdy maroon canes and splendid dark foliage coming right to the base of the flower. The buds and half-open flowers, though small, are quite attractive, with deep yellow base color edged with capsicum red. Petals are rather short but have a brisk flare at the tip. 'Charisma's' color changes are less jarring than those of 'Rumba'—it deepens to Orient red, thus remaining in the scarlet range—but its petals recurve and quill badly and then fade to mottled gray with reddish edges. The loss of form, fading and failure to shed spent petals are all traceable to 'Rumba.' Apparently the gentler influence of 'Zorina' was unable to overcome these defects.

**Bahia** ('Rumba' x 'Tropicana,' AARS 1974) is a much taller plant than 'Charisma,' no doubt due to its Hybrid Tea parent 'Tropicana.' The plant is variable, with some strong canes and some weak twiggy ones, all of which tend to be bare at the bottom because of susceptibility to blackspot. The flowers, Dutch vermilion with a rosy overtone and pleasingly ruffled, are sometimes borne singly and more often in tight, many-headed clusters. Almost as soon as they open, the flowers begin to change to Delft rose, then gray-pink, and remain hanging on the stems like wads of used cleansing tissue streaked with cold cream and makeup.

**Redgold** ([('Karl Herbst' x 'Masquerade') x 'Faust'] x 'Piccadilly,' AARS 1971) has distinguished grandparents in 'Peace' and 'Independence.' Its resemblance to

'Rumba's' children must be a case of guilt by association. The plants have beautiful glossy foliage, dense and clean, reaching to the base of the bud. The buds, chrome yellow with coral edges, deepen to near orange with red margins. Flowers are scant petaled, hardly more than semidouble, and are loose and irregular in form. Petals recurve badly and fade to gray mottled with dull pink, a most distressing contrast with newly open flowers.

It seems axiomatic that roses should be as beautiful in maturity as they are in the bud stage, if only because the life of a bud is short in comparison with the duration of fully developed flowers. Dealers do a disservice to gardeners by offering varieties that are grossly defective in this respect. Judges who give faulty roses a seal of commendation are equally to blame.

With **Circus** ('Fandango' x 'Pinocchio,' AARS 1956) we return to the list of favorite roses. From its pedigree, it would be safe to predict a superlative variety. 'Fandango' descends from 'Charlotte Armstrong,' offspring of the patriarch 'Crimson Glory,' while 'Pinocchio' is a child of 'Eva.' 'Circus' is a jolly plant, always noticed by visitors and usually evoking a smile of pleasure. The plant is tall with vigorous maroon canes clothed to the ground with dense, glossy, dark green foliage. The flowers are large enough to pass for a HT if disbudded but it would be a pity to disrupt the delightful ruffly effect of the loose clusters. 'Circus' is much like 'Sutter's Gold' in coloring. It opens light buffy yellow, edged at first with a border of muted rose madder which progressively suffuses the whole flower. The reverse is carmine red. The interplay of color between newly opened and mature flowers is lighthearted and stimulating. The base tone of 'Circus' is much like that of 'Golden Fleece,' a much dwarfer plant, so the two could be grouped if a restrained repetition-with-variation harmony is wanted. When you reflect that the ancestor of all yellow-and-red bicolors was the fugitive five-petaled *Rosa foetida,* you are impelled to salute the generations of patient breeders who have transmuted its blood into an everblooming rose with the staunch constitution, disease resistance and richly diverse color harmony of 'Circus.'

## YELLOW FLORIBUNDAS

Though yellow Floribundas are few numerically, it is pleasant to be able to give high recommendation to three. The purest yellow is **Yellow Cushion** ('Fandango' x 'Pinocchio,' 1966) which, as you will notice, has exactly the same parents as 'Circus.' 'Yellow Cushion,' however, is not a bicolor but a delectable primrose yellow, the best harmonizer in the garden—far better than white, which can be glaring in full sunlight. This clear light yellow is unfortunately rare in flowers which, undoubtedly in deference to insect preferences, major in dandelion yellow or taxicab chrome. The flowers of 'Yellow Cushion' are of medium size, full petaled, of beautifully smooth texture, enlivened with a glow of amber in the depths and opening slowly to show a generous golden heart. 'Yellow Cushion' has a constitutional quirk that must be humored: it will not endure full sun on its roots. A row of plants at the extreme south end of a bed in the BBG shrank into oblivion, while those located between taller plants, although drawn tall in search of light, survived and bloomed. Treat 'Yellow Cushion' like a lily or clematis: head in the sun, roots in the shade. If you can place it behind a low wall to its south, or give it a border of dwarf box or clipped germander, with an insulating

**Golden Fleece.**

mulch over its roots, you can enjoy the gentle charm of these light yellow roses all summer. Some of the canes bear rather crowded clusters of bloom. Occasionally a flower is borne singly: this will be a choice subject for a small arrangement at the side of your reading chair, for 'Yellow Cushion' is a rose that invites close and leisurely enjoyment.

**Golden Fleece** ('Diamond Jubilee' x 'Yellow Sweetheart,' 1955) is a rarity: a yellow rose that blooms without pause in the hottest weather and boasts foliage that is highly resistant to fungus diseases. It is of medium height and carries its profusion of flowers on erect branching stems. The color is not clear yellow but more nearly amber with an apricot flush in the heart of newly opened flowers. It is a soft, compatible color, especially appealing by moon- or candlelight. The flowers are neither as firm nor as full petaled as those of 'Yellow Cushion.' They are loosely double, not in the least remarkable for form but effective as a mass of ruffly bloom. 'Golden Fleece' makes its gentle statement not on the basis of brilliance but because of the profligate generosity of its flowering.

**Courvoisier** ('Elizabeth of Glamis' x 'Casanova,' 1970) has 'Spartan' and 'Queen Elizabeth' as grandparents and 'Independence' as a great-grandparent, all three wearing 'Eva's' family crest. Like many yellow roses, 'Courvoisier' takes a summer siesta so prolonged that the impatient gardener may begin to wonder whether it justifies its garden space. With the coming of cool September nights, it sends up tall stout canes clothed with shiny foliage and bearing a profusion of large, fully double flowers. These are corn yellow with a rich tint of apricot in the depths. Since most of the blooms come singly, this is an outstanding rose for cutting, as its many petals and firm substance give it great staying power. 'Courvoisier' is an oddly reminiscent rose. In form and to a lesser extent in coloring, it resembles the epoch-making 'Soleil d'Or' though it lacks the tangerine tones in the latter's newly opened flowers. Again, the cupped outer segments enclosing a swirl of tightly packed shorter petals recall the silky Bourbon roses popular in the early and mid-1800s. One of these may be familiar: 'Souvenir de la Malmaison' (1843) named in remembrance of flower-loving Empress Josephine's rose garden some thirty years after her death.

**Courvoisier.** The form is that of a Bourbon Rose.

There is nothing melancholy about 'Courvoisier.' It is a joyful recreation of a past era in colors Josephine couldn't have dreamed of. To top off its attractions, 'Courvoisier' has a strong rose fragrance combined with that of spiced tea brewed with cloves and citrus rind and stirred with a cinnamon stick.

## LAVENDER FLORIBUNDAS

The heading should be singular. There is only one of consequence: **Angel Face** (['Circus' x 'Lavender Pinocchio'] x 'Sterling Silver,' AARS 1969). The three-inch

**Angel Face.**

flower is quite charming: its gracefully rippled flowers open flat to display an unusual color pattern. The ground color is dusky mauve, edged in the young flower with a ribbon of bright Persian rose or, in dressmakers' terms, shocking pink. The border fades first, then the ground, which ends in a drab gray-lavender. The fragrance is uncommonly intense: rich old rose laced with a hint of spice. If the plant had a good constitution, it would make a harmonious companion, both in color and scale, for 'Yellow Cushion.' However, 'Angel Face' is so abjectly disposed to mildew and blackspot that plants are entirely defoliated by late summer. The plant lacks sufficient stamina to compensate for summer dieback by vigorous spring and fall growth. Some of the plants seem to be holding their own but not gaining; others are plainly losing ground. It is unfortunate that this pleasing little rose isn't furnished with a plant as strong as its appeal.

## Red Floribundas

Considering the oversupply of red Hybrid Teas, produced in great numbers each year presumably in response to an insatiable demand, it is strange that there are so few deep red Floribundas. One reason may be that none of the available varieties is suitable for cutting. The clusters are too crowded and too short stemmed to permit the gathering of single flowers, so they can't be enjoyed in the house under artificial light as HTs can. In addition, deep colors tend to merge into shadow after sundown. As a result, dark red roses have no landscape value for those who like to use their terraces in the evening.

A discussion of red Floribundas must start with **Baby**

**Chateau** ('Aroma' x ['Eva' x 'Ami Quinard'], 1936). This is so plainly showing deterioration from age, with crumpled, deformed flowers, that it is perhaps unkind to point it out. On the chance that you may catch an acceptable bloom, and because of the variety's inestimable value in rose breeding, you may want to look at the two plants located midway along the east side of the third central bed in the BBG. Flowers are semidouble and deep oxblood red with a curious smoky bloom, almost like a dusting of brownish pollen, which dims the color. The same dulling haze appears on a red Moss Rose, 'Deuil de Paul Fontaine,' declining after more than one hundred years. It is probably a symptom of weakness in both cases rather than a true representation of the flower in its youthful prime.

**Donald Prior** (unnamed seedling x 'D. T. Poulsen,' 1938) is only two years younger than 'Baby Chateau' but still appears flourishing. The plant is rather slight, with thin canes, but the foliage is clean and ample. The semidouble flowers are rich cardinal red with shadings of oxblood. They open wide to show a generous mound of bright yellow stamens, very effective against the dark petals. This is a serviceable variety, not spectacular, but welcome in a color range that is so scantily filled.

**Red Pinocchio** (unnamed 'Yellow Pinocchio' seedling x 'Donald Prior,' 1947) is cardinal red, the same basic color as 'Donald Prior' but with a brownish cast and matt finish that reduces brilliance. Even though they are freely produced, the tight clusters of small flowers have little visual impact. The variety is so extremely subject to mildew that foliage is usually crumpled and even the flower stalks and buds are gray and distorted.

**Europeana** ('Ruth Leuwerick' x 'Rosemary Rose,' AARS 1968) is far and away the best of the dark red

Floribundas. It flowers with the utmost generosity even in midsummer, bearing its ruffled blooms in huge, sometimes top-heavy clusters. The color is glowing cherry red with a slightly deeper currant-red bloom. The petals have the same velvety surface as those of 'Donald Prior' but the overall tone is much brighter. The plant tends to grow overly tall, with canes too limber to support the weight of the massed flowers, and should be shortened quite severely when spent flowers are removed. Foliage is glossy and disease resistant. The plant seems to be so steeped in redness that all its new growth is maroon: the leaves, when fully mature, retain a hint of dark red under their green overtone. The flowers are semidouble and loosely formed, useless for cutting because of the congested clusters and short individual stems. 'Europeana' has a strong tea fragrance with a rich fruit-and-wine undertone, the pungent aroma that rises when you pour a good dollop of Madeira into hot orange sauce for duck.

## White Floribundas

White roses, given the slightest illumination from porch lights, hurricane lamps or moonlight, continue to be effective at night long after dark-toned flowers have lost identity. For this reason they are especially valuable to those who enjoy outdoor dining.

**Saratoga** ('White Bouquet' x 'Princess White,' AARS 1964) heads the list of white Floribundas for landscape effect. The flowers cover the plant without pause from late May to killing frost. The plant is fairly tall and somewhat lax, with canes just limber enough to arch over at the top to form a gracefully rounded bush. On first opening, the buds have a firm spiral center with a warming hint of yellow at the base. The mature flowers, soon opening wide and measuring 3½ inches across, are semidouble and lightly ruffled. The large overlapping clusters, broad but airy looking, make a telling display in the garden.

**Evening Star** (1974) has truly noble parents: 'Saratoga,' the best white Floribunda, and the magnificently formed but sparse-flowering HT 'White Masterpiece.' Its buds are as beautiful as those of 'Saratoga' but somewhat larger. Whereas 'Saratoga's' open flowers are thin in texture and individually fleeting, those of 'Evening Star' are as smooth and thick as gardenia petals, with substance so heavy that their spiral form is prolonged for days. A yellow light is present in the depths; in addition, in cool cloudy weather the flowers take on an ethereal wash of clear green, the refreshing tint that enhances the purity of white snapdragons and stock. 'Evening Star' is a heartbreaker: as it grows in the BBG, it is so severely injured by fungus diseases that the plants are barely holding their own. It manages to put on a show of its surpassingly lovely flowers in autumn— breathtakingly, achingly beautiful even on canes with contorted gray, spotted leaves or none. It is possible that 'Evening Star' might fare better in areas with low humidity or where summers are cooler. Meanwhile, for yearning gardeners in less favored climates, it is hoped that the breeder will repeat the cross in an effort to give 'Evening Star' the sturdy plant its exceptional beauty deserves.

**Summer Snow** (1938) is a dwarf sport of a climber of the same name, thus giving a reverse twist to the usual process. It is a low plant, compact and flowery. Its small white ruffled flowers, borne in profuse clusters close to the plant, have a trace of light yellow on first opening.

**Evening Star** has flowers of classic perfection, surpassing most Hybrid Teas in form.

The foliage is light green and remarkably free of disease. 'Summer Snow' gives much the same effect as 'The Fairy,' though on a somewhat larger scale, and would make an equally good if taller border.

**Ivory Fashion** ('Sonata' x 'Fashion,' AARS 1959) must have surprised its breeder, who crossed two shrimp pink roses and got a near-white. 'Ivory Fashion' is a tall Floribunda with little to recommend it in the way of habit or disease resistance. It tends to be leggy and its shanks may be bare by fall. However, its flowers have such individual grace, such refinement of finish that they can hardly be equaled for elegance and restraint. The flowers are large and semidouble, cream-colored in bud, fading to ivory white but retaining a flush of yellow in the center. The singular charm of the flower, and the feature that commends it for close inspection, lies in its heart. The filaments, the threadlike processes that support the pollen-bearing anthers, are bright red-gold, a feature usually reserved for single roses such as 'Innocence.' The dark strands circling the deep gold stigmata give the effect of eyelashes and lend an animated, wide-awake look to the flower. 'Ivory Fashion' is a fairly steady but not lavish performer, sufficiently tolerant of hot weather to earn its keep throughout the summer. In autumn its flowers take on tints of pink and yellow, as luminous and subtly blended as the highlights of a pearl.

# 6
# Old Roses

If you visit the BBG rose garden in late May when the shrub rose borders flood the air with sweetness, a profligate wave of perfume augmented by lilacs and wisteria just beyond the boundaries, you will think you have been transported to the Islands of the Blessed. At this time of overwhelming fragrance, you will wonder why everyone doesn't grow old roses. Come back in August when the borders are barren of color, when foliage is mildewed or rusty, and you will understand why the cult of old roses is not a common addiction. As a fact, we are spoiled by the repeat-flowering modern roses and tend to forget that a vast majority of our unquestioned garden favorites—daffodils, tulips, Oriental poppies, iris, peonies, gladiolus as well as flowering shrubs and trees—have only one period of bloom and in some cases take themselves away below ground without even a clump of foliage to fill their site.

It's hard to define the charm of old roses. They may bloom only once but that display covers a good six weeks without pause. If their colors lack the fiery brilliance of today's orange and vermilion roses, they extend the range into violet and purple and indulge in fantastically striped combinations not found in modern varieties. They are threaded through history, art, religion and legend, from the quartered bloom on the Great Seal of England to the delicately striped rose named for Fair Rosamund, beloved of Henry II, to the parti-colored pink-and-white rose that symbolized the union of the warring houses of York and Lancaster. Beyond every other consideration is the grace of fragrance, so varied, so powerful, so intoxicatingly rich that its memory will haunt the air long after the flowers that breathed it are past.

Happily it is seldom necessary to make an either/or decision. For the owner of a moderately spacious garden, the solution is easy: plant the lacquered scentless modern beauties in the center beds and use the old roses in a sheltering border or train them along a boundary fence or wall. In most cases, the modern roses bloom later than the old varieties, so there is only a short period of overlapping when strident colors might clash with gentler ones.

Not all old roses are shrubs; not all shrub roses are old. Since there is no more exact or inclusive word, the terms "old rose" and "shrub rose" are here used loosely as a way of differentiating them from modern garden roses such as Hybrid Teas and Floribundas.

A dedication to propagating old roses and making them available to collectors is more an expression of love than a means of getting rich. Understandably, few specialist rose growers have the resolution to continue the struggle against ever-increasing expenses for labor, shipping and taxes. Each time their ranks are thinned by retirement, scores of treasures are lost. The BBG plans to build up its collection of old roses in an effort to preserve as many as possible for the use of students and—perhaps more important—to serve as a reservoir of budwood for nurserymen who may catch Old Rose Fever in the future. For this reason some outstanding varieties growing in the BBG will be described even though they are not at present commercially available. These roses will be marked with a dagger (†). Nurserymen may be persuaded to add to their lists if gardeners ask for the varieties that stir their interest.

A two-year attempt to unscramble the old roses in the BBG produced few certain identifications but roused a consuming interest that spurred the production of this book. The first shock that confronts an earnest researcher is the discovery that there is no definitive, fully illustrated monograph on species roses and their ancient varieties and hybrids. When you consider the exhaustive treatises on what rose lovers must consider minor plants, it is quite incredible that no comprehensive study has been made of roses. There's Maw's masterly monograph on crocus, with 326 pages of exquisitely detailed color plates and enlarged dissections of reproductive organs and other diagnostic aids; there's Dykes on iris, again with superb color plates; Hall on tulips, with color portraits that insure instant recognition; Stern on snowdrops and leucojums; Lee on azaleas; Hume on hollies and camellias—and yet there's no one book that students can turn to for clear and authoritative depiction of rose species and how to tell one from another. It is necessary to pick up a hint here and a clue there, often lacking in conclusive detail, sometimes contradictory. In the event, close observation of the old roses growing in the BBG—

those whose identification was unquestioned—led to a rough-and-ready key which is offered below for the use of inquiring amateurs.

When it comes to identifying ancient hybrids, the lack of an illustrated register is keenly felt. It is easy enough to say what a variety is *not*. When a pink Moss Rose is labeled 'Belle de Crécy,' a cerise-to-purple Gallica, you know that something has gone awry, but it's quite another matter to put a name to the pink Moss. Even with the most studious comparison of descriptions in Graham Stuart Thomas's *The Old Shrub Roses*, Bobbink & Atkins's 1940 catalogue and a sheaf of Tillotson and Kern catalogues dating back twenty years, it was not possible to identify a number of similar pink Mosses nor to sort out the purple Gallicas. Heights and colors vary widely in different soils and climates and in the observer's eye, for one man's crimson is another's magenta. There remain many charming puzzles in the BBG shrub borders but unless we can import Mr. Thomas for a season, it is not likely that they will be given their rightful names.

Over the centuries, the original rose species have interbred, at first crossed by bees, more recently by man. The resulting bloodlines are so complex that it is often impossible to unscramble them. However, it is usually possible to identify the predominating strain even if the more recessive ancestors remain a puzzle. To add to the confusion, nurseries sometimes send out misnamed material obtained by them in good faith. Caretakers of public and botanic gardens, not necessarily trained in taxonomy, are apt to assume that the rose they receive is the rose they ordered. In some cases a plant dies and is replaced by another without changing the label. All too frequently, the named variety is enveloped and choked out by the understock—usually *Rosa multiflora*—which remains as an impostor behind the rightful tenant's label. A trip to the New York Botanical Garden, made in the hope of clinching some identifications, turned up the same confusion—and the added observation that the soil in the corner beds where the old roses are planted was trampled hard, as if many people had stepped among the plants for a closer look, a breath of perfume or a photograph. If the caretakers of the rose garden recognize the packed soil as evidence of strong public interest, perhaps they will respond with more sympathetic treatment of the old roses.

It is hoped that the botanical distinctions that follow will help the student of old roses to establish some identities and enable the gardener to form some idea of what to expect in the way of size and habit.

Since the Gallicas and Damasks seem to cause more confusion than the other species, let's take them up first. If you weather this study of identification, the rest should be easy.

First it is necessary to confront two botanical terms: *receptacle* and *sepal*. The receptacle is the swollen process at the upper end of a flower stalk, the base to which all parts of a flower are fixed. It encloses the ovary and, as fertilized seeds mature, becomes the highly colored fruit, the rose hip (or hep, a form you may encounter in British horticultural literature). The shape of the receptacle and the distribution of glands (fleshy, sticky protuberances) are often the clinching diagnostic keys to identification. The term *sepal* is likely to be more familiar. Sepals are the outermost series of leaflike parts of a flower.

In roses, sepals are green structures that grow from the upper edges of the receptacle and serve to cover and protect the developing flower bud. The length of the sepals in relation to the bud, their margins (entire or slashed), the angle they assume under the open flower and the degree of mossiness (a proliferation of enlarged glands) may be significant in indicating the probable bloodlines of a rose. You should also keep in mind that many of the old roses are hybrids so any statement about them must be prefaced with the qualification *usually*.

## Rosa Gallica and Rosa Damascena

Often you can recognize a Gallica at a glance. It is characteristic of the species to send out short suckers from the base, making a tight thicket of erect, largely unbranched stems as stiff as broomstraws. Stems are densely covered with fine bristles with an occasional hooked prickle on the older wood. The flowers are small to mid-sized, borne sometimes in small clusters but more often singly and held upright on stout stalks. Buds are round and blunt with sepals not projecting far beyond their tips. The receptacle is bowl-shaped or, more graphically, like an acorn with its top sliced off. Foliage is firm, thick, dark green on top and paler beneath. The sides of each leaflet tend to rise at an angle to the midrib which in turn arches upward in a bow. The leafstalk and its extension, the rachis, also describe an arc, giving the plant a wingy look as if it were poised to spring into flight.

John Gerard in his great *Herball* of 1597 describes **Rosa gallica** as it grew in his London garden: "The red Rose groweth very low in respect of the former [*Rosa* *alba*]: the stalks are shorter, smoother, and browner of colour . . . the floures grow on the top of the branches, consisting of many leaves of a perfect red colour. . . ." If Gerard had used a hand lens, he would have discovered that the brown color of the stem was due partly to bristles and partly to myriads of tiny pinheaded glands, red or pinkish, translucent and sticky, which cover not only the stems but every part of the plant except the petals. These glands occur on the flower stalks, receptacles and sepals, on the leafstalks and veins on the underside of the leaflets and *even between the teeth that edge the margins.* If you hold a leaflet against the light and examine it with a lens, you will see little points of red light at the bases of the teeth. This is the most reliable diagnostic key to *Rosa gallica* and its hybrids. Sticky glands on the canes presumably serve to discourage crawling insects such as ants which might otherwise climb the stalk and rob the flower of its nectar without pollinating it. Their presence on the leaf margins appears to be sheer exuberance.

Gallica roses have an astounding color span, lacking white but ranging from pink and deep rose to a red close to scarlet, through unique shades of brownish maroon, mauve, lilac, violet and purple, sometimes self-colored, sometimes exhibiting extraordinary combinations of two or more of these colors in stripes, bands and shadings.

While the Gallica features are fresh in mind, we should compare them with the Damasks before going on to describe the varieties. Everything about Damask roses is soft—except of course for the large hooked prickles that arm its stems. Canes are lax, often arching to the ground. Foliage is gray-green, downy and drooping. The flowers, borne in large clusters on somewhat flexuous stalks, are silky in finish and embrace a rather limited

*Rosa damascena.* The characteristic urn-shaped receptacle is well shown in the bud at extreme right.

but delectable range of colors from white and blush to deeper shades of rose. Buds are gracefully tapered with long flyaway sepals, often feathered or slashed. The flowers are intensely sweet—more strongly scented than a fresh-cut Gallica—but the fragrance dissipates when the petals are dried. Flower stalks, receptacle and sepals are sparingly furnished with glandular bristles. The best mark of identification of the Damask rose is the receptacle: it is shaped like a tall slender vase with a distinct incurve at the neck, an outline instantly recognizable and totally unlike the chunky hemisphere of the Gallicas.

*Rosa gallica* and **R. damascena** vie for the distinction of being the first rose to be depicted in art, at least art that has survived to the present day. The fresco on the house wall in Cnossos, Crete, is estimated as dating from around 2000 B.C. It depicts a freely imagined rose, brick red in color, with six petals instead of the actual five, and leaves with only three leaflets, all borne on vinelike canes that swirl in animated loops and spirals. There's no doubt that it is intended as a rose even though it is so highly stylized for decorative effect that its identity can't be established with certainty. Since both these ancient species have their roots in history, it seems only fair to let them share the honor without any attempt to give one precedence over the other.

## Rosa Gallica Varieties

*Rosa gallica,* the French Rose, Rose of Provins or Red Rose of Lancaster, has two especially famous varieties: *Rosa gallica officinalis* and its striped sport, *R. g. versicolor* or 'Rosa Mundi.' The term "officinalis" indicates that some portion of the plant, dried or otherwise preserved, was regularly stocked by apothecaries for use as medicine. If the medicinal properties were wholly imaginary, at least the administration of herbal concoctions satisfied the need of anxious relatives to do something for a sick or injured patient. As noted in the introduction, the Dog Rose, *Rosa canina,* was carried to Britain in the baggage of Roman legions in the belief that its root was an antidote for the bite of a mad dog. An equally venerable fantasy gave rose petals, especially those of red roses, the power to cure tuberculosis—a clear case of sympathetic magic by which the color of the petals was supposed to transfer itself to the pale cheeks of the sufferer. As late as 1694, William Westmacott, Physician, wrote in A *Scripture Herbal* that "Conserve and Sugar of Roses, of old, were celebrated Remedies in Consumptions, insomuch as some emaciated and ptisical Bodies have been said to have been restored, or long preserv'd by the Use of them; so still these days doth the Conserve (especially if three or four Year old) keep its famous Reputation among Practitioners. . . ." John Parkinson in his *Paradisi in Sole* (1619) proclaimed the merits of *Rosa Anglica rubra* whose description, closely tallying with that of Gerard, proves it a Gallica: "(it) abideth low and shooteth forth many branches from the roote. . . ." Parkinson astutely observes that the fresh flower "is not comparable to the excellencie of the damaske Rose, yet this Rose being well dryed and well kept, will hold both colour and sent longer than the damaske, be it never so well kept." It is a recognized fact that the fragrance of the Damask rose is not persistent, whereas that of *R. gallica officinalis*, though not so sweet when freshly gathered, increases in intensity as it dries.

According to tradition, *R. g. officinalis* was collected in the Valley of Damascus in the early thirteenth century by a Crusader, King Tibaut IV of Navarre, who brought it back to Provins, a town southeast of Paris. This variety, with its extraordinary property of retaining its color and fragrance, gave rise to a great industry which flourished around Provins until the middle of the nineteenth century, supplying rose conserve and dried petals to Europe and Britain for the use of apothecaries, cooks, confectioners and perfumers.

As Parkinson noted, *R. gallica officinalis* "abideth low and shooteth forth many branches from the roote" in the manner characteristic of its species. The flower is mid-sized and semidouble. Its glowing rose-red color is set off by a generous heart of golden stamens. While the fresh flower is not so fragrant as a Damask, it is the preeminent choice of gardeners who wish to impart lasting color and scent to potpourri, sugared rose petals or other confections.

In 1455, *Rosa gallica officinalis* took an active role in the course of history. It was chosen as the symbol of the faction that supported the Lancastrian claim to the English throne, while the Yorkists selected a white rose, *Rosa alba*, as their emblem. The picking of the roses is recounted in *The First Part of Henry the Sixth*, act II, scene iv. It ends with a prophecy:

> This brawl today
> Grown to this faction in the Temple-garden,
> Shall send between the red rose and the white
> A thousand souls to death and deadly night.

The prophecy proved to be an understatement: the Wars of the Roses lasted thirty years and cost many times a thousand lives. It is fitting that the end of hostilities was signaled by the choice of still another rose, the pink-and-white *R. damascena versicolor* which is described on pages 113–114.

Another Gallica variety, *Rosa gallica versicolor*, embodies an older and more romantic story. It is a sport of the rose-red *R. gallica* and is believed to have been found in a Syrian garden and, like *R. g. officinalis*, carried to England by a returning Crusader. It was named 'Rosa Mundi' in tribute to Fair Rosamund, beloved of Henry II. The attachment was a costly one for Henry: it alienated his powerful queen, Eleanor of Aquitaine. Despite her vengeful jealousy, Henry resolutely maintained his fidelity to Rosamund until her death in 1176. 'Rosa Mundi,' like its parent, is vigorous and upright, bearing its lovely flowers on sturdy stems well above the foliage. It is a magnificent garden subject, standing high on the list of outstanding old roses. The flowers are white or blush with bold irregular stripes grading from pale pink to deep rose-red. If Rosamund had as perfect a complexion, she well deserved the epithet "Fair." It is pleasing to think that after more than eight hundred years, the memory of her beauty and loving heart still lives in the rose that bears her name.

Since we have been discussing Gallicas that date back to the Crusades, we may be permitted to speak of more recent garden forms as "modern"—meaning that they originated in the early part of the past century. Among them are some of the maddest of the Mad Gallicas, as they are termed with good reason. Their range of color is unique; their fanciful assortment of striped forms must be seen to be believed.

**Cardinal de Richelieu** dates from 1840. The plant is vigorous and spreads by suckers into a broad dense thicket. The flowers are fragrant, very full and of moderate size, but produced with great abundance during their one long flowering season. The exposed end of the fat bud is sharp pink and, when seen among open flowers, seems to have strayed in from another variety. As the bud slowly opens, the tightly massed petals pass from pink to cerise and then to a marvelously rich deep violet, enlivened by a white base on each petal which is disclosed as the flower opens more fully. In some lights, the flower appears almost blue; in others, it is as deep and bloomy as a Concord grape. With age, the short segments curl backwards to form a ball so light and fluffy that it looks as if it might be composed of feathers instead of petals. The sumptuous tone of the flowers and their modest size make them delightful companions for delicate candy-pink Moss Roses either in the garden or in a choice Victorian vase.

'Cardinal de Richelieu' is not commercially available at this writing but, in accordance with the BBG's plan, budwood has been sent to Tillotson's Roses for propagation. Write early to reserve your plant as this outstanding variety is certain to be in demand. We hope it escapes the notice of the sharpers who advertise their dubious wares in unscrupulous newspapers and magazines. They'd use screaming headlines: ASTONISH YOUR NEIGHBORS! BE THE FIRST TO GROW A BLUE ROSE! Well, you can—but don't expect a gigantic indigo 'Peace.' For all their bizarre coloring, the Mad Gallicas are relatively small flowers. They appeal to those who find charm in collecting cameos, netsuke or snuff boxes rather than outsize paintings of soup cans or giant plastic replicas of hamburgers. They need the company of their own kind and would be miserably overshadowed if forced to compete in a bed of modern Hybrid Teas.

†**Captain Williams** is not a strong-growing plant, at least as it fares in the BBG. Its flowers are larger than those of 'Cardinal de Richelieu' and go through nearly as spectacular color changes, from a magenta-rose bud to a cyclamen purple middle age, ending as petunia purple. The overtone is warmer than that of the Cardinal and closer to the red side of violet, an intensely brilliant color found in the overskirts of purple fuchsias. If the plant makes enough new shoots so that one or two can be spared without endangering the plant, budwood will go to Tillotson's.

†**Désirée Parmentier** is more sedate in its coloring,

being bright cerise pink with a slight darkening to magenta-rose as it ages. The flower is large and flat with a good golden heart. The plant lacks the period charm of most of its kin and might in fact be mistaken for a Floribunda—but as it flowers only once, there is no reason to plant it in preference to a modern repeat-flowering variety.

†**The Bishop (L'Evêque)** is another of the velvety dark Gallicas. It opens a bright orchid purple and matures to petunia purple with a deep violet bloom, sometimes washed with gray or near-blue. Some of the petals retain patches of the youthful cerise coloring, giving a very sportive effect. The flowers open quite flat in a way that displays their vivid color to best advantage. Since this is a fairly good grower, it is expected that budwood will find its way to Tillotson's in time.

**Belle de Crécy,** as grown at the New York Botanical Garden, answers Graham Thomas's description of that variety. The plant is a little lax—an uncommon fault among Gallicas, possibly indicating hybridity—with slender arching canes clothed in dull gray-green leaves. The cerise buds quickly open to fair-sized flowers of plum violet with dashes of fuchsia and purple, a dark but regal combination of velvety tones. In the mature flower, the petals reflex and reveal a pale green center. Many flowers are imperfect but the mass effect of the flower-laden bush is sumptuous, as is its perfume.

## DAMASK ROSES

Richard Hakluyt, in *The Principall Navigations, Voiages, Traffiques and Defcoueries of the English Nation,* 1559, tells us that the Damask Rose was brought to En-

gland "in time of Memory . . . by Doctour Linaker, King
Henry the seuenth and King Henrie the eight's Phyfi-
cian." (Elizabethan English, with its transposition of *u*
and *v* and the long *s*, has great period flavor but it will be
modernized slightly in the ensuing passages for ease in
reading.) Dr. Thomas Linacre, born in 1460, was a mul-
tifaceted Renaissance man, an eminent Greek scholar,
educator and writer who studied medicine in various
universities on the Continent and who received his degree in Padua. Since almost all remedies of the time
were of herbal origin, a physician by necessity was well
versed in botany. A Physicke Garden, a collection of
herbs used in healing, was an essential part of every
medical school. It is entirely possible that the student
Linacre noticed the Damask Rose and brought it with
him when he returned to England to practice medicine.
Assuming that he graduated in his mid- to late twenties,
we can estimate that the rose reached England in the
late 1480s, where it gained rapid and wide acceptance.

The herbalists Gerard and Parkinson grew Damask
Roses. It was an especial favorite of Parkinson's who
wrote that it was "of the most excellent sweet pleasant
sent, far surpassing all other Roses or Flowers, being
neyther heady nor too strong, nor stuffing or unpleasant
sweet, as many other flowers." Parkinson quite discern-
ingly recognized "The party coloured Rose, of some
York and Lancaster" as a variety of Damask. (It is *Rosa
damascena versicolor,* given the name of York and Lancaster Rose in 1551.) "This Rose in the forme and order
of the growing, is neerest unto the ordinary damaske
rose, both for stemme, branch, leafe and flower, the difference consisting in this, that the flower (being of the
same largenesse and doublenesse as the damask rose)
hath the one halfe of it, sometimes of a pale whitish

colour, and the other halfe, of a paler damaske colour then the ordinary; this happeneth so many times, and sometimes also the flower hath divers stripes, and marks in it, as one leafe white, or striped with white, and the other halfe blush, or striped with blush. . . ." This would seem to leave no leaf unturned, but Parkinson goes on for some time in describing every possible variation. He must have admired it strongly to have given it such minute observation.

The 'York and Lancaster' rose is charming in a modest way, with its soft coloring and irregular form—and, unfortunately, a rather weak constitution. There is sometimes confusion between this rose and the other ancient parti-colored rose, *Rosa gallica versicolor*, or 'Rosa Mundi,' but the latter is boldly striped with deep rose or crimson on a pale ground, a far more dramatic contrast than the gentle half-pink, half-white 'York and Lancaster.'

Damask Roses seem to have remained fairly stable until the early years of the nineteenth century when there was a revival of interest in breeding them.

**Mme. Hardy** was introduced in 1832 and still is unsurpassed for beauty among white roses. The bush is somewhat taller than is usual with Damasks but has the typical lax canes and drooping gray-green foliage. If left to grow naturally, the canes sometimes fall away too sharply, leaving the center of the bush hollow. This can usually be remedied by tying all the canes together about three feet above ground level—or if this isn't sufficient support, by using an unobtrusive short stake. When tied this way, the canes will arch gracefully under their load of blossoms yet not pull too far apart, exposing the bare center.

The bud of 'Mme. Hardy' agrees with Damask specifi-

**Mme. Hardy.** A superb example of a quartered rose with petals
nested in four to six sections.

cations: the receptacle is an elongated ovoid with a marked identation just below the sepals. However, the flower is too full and too formal to be undiluted Damask. Graham Stuart Thomas, the ultimate authority on old roses, thinks 'Mme. Hardy' may have R. *centifolia* as well as Gallica blood. Whatever the ingredients, the result is pure enchantment. As the round buds part their long feathered sepals, they show a faint trace of palest blush pink in the newly opened flower. This quickly passes to white—not dead white as in the HP 'Frau Karl Druschki' but warmed with a hint of ivory. In their best form, the flowers are precisely quartered, that is, the petals are arranged in four equal divisions, each cupped petal nested in a larger one below it, exactly like graduated measuring spoons. This is the pattern of quartering that appears in the heraldic rose of England and in woodcarvings in old churches and manor houses. The center of 'Mme. Hardy' is somewhat open and shows not the expected yellow stamens but the tips of pale green carpels which add just the right accent to set off the perfection of the flower. It is sometimes difficult to hit on an accurate description of the scent of a flower but this one is easy: it smells exactly like Pond's cold cream.

Any rose that follows 'Mme. Hardy' is inevitably an anticlimax. **Marie Louise** is a less beautiful Damask hybrid, not commercially available at present but of such historical interest that it deserves at least a mention. It was reputedly raised at Malmaison, the deposed Empress Josephine's country residence, in 1813, a year before her death. Josephine's passion for roses, at the time an unfashionable flower, led her to try to collect every rose to be found on the Continent and in England. In addition to searching out existing varieties, Josephine's chief plantsman, André du Pont, was the first Frenchman to undertake an extensive program of raising new roses from seed, something that had been done on a limited scale in the Netherlands. Among Josephine's inestimable services in popularizing the rose was her choice of Pierre Joseph Redouté as official artist for the Malmaison collection. Although Redouté's sumptuous portrait gallery, *Les Roses*, appeared after Josephine's death, it stands as a monument to her love of the flower.

'Marie Louise' probably owes its enormously full petalage to an infusion of *R. centifolia* blood. Its flowers are so heavy that they weigh down the plant's long flexuous canes, from which the flowers turn upwards and develop crook necks. Weak necks and an undeniably magenta-rose color were the norm in Josephine's day and would not have been judged defects as they are today. The recorded date and place of origin are in conflict with its name and give rise to serious doubts: it is highly unlikely that Josephine would have named a rose, or permitted one to be named, for Marie Louise, the treacherous Austrian archduchess who replaced Josephine as Napoleon's empress. Perhaps it was named after Josephine's death as a way of currying favor with the new regime? For the sake of poetic justice to Josephine, who contributed so vitally to the development and appreciation of the rose, one can hope that 'Marie Louise' was indeed produced in Josephine's lifetime and that she enjoyed its opulence and ravishing fragrance.

The BBG grows a modern Damask hybrid which is as arresting as it is curious. While not commercially available, it is something to look for in future if you have a taste for novelty. It is named **Oratam** for a seventeenth-century Indian chief of the Lenni-Lenape tribe of northern New Jersey. The rose, introduced in 1939, is a cross between *Rosa damascena* and 'Souvenir de Claudius Pernet' (1920), a yellow rose famous in its day and much used in breeding. It was named in memory of one of two sons of the breeder Pernet-Ducher, both of whom were killed in World War I. If you recall, it was Pernet who, after years of patient effort, managed to get viable seed by using pollen from the Persian Yellow, a double form of *R. foetida*, on a rose-red Hybrid Perpetual, 'Antoine Ducher.' The one fertile seedling that resulted was mated with Hybrid Teas and produced 'Soleil d'Or,' the direct ancestor of all our yellow-red bicolors. 'Soleil d'Or' is described on page 40. 'Oratam' has little about it that suggests a Damask except its entrancing perfume which combines rich old-rose fragrance with the scent of sun-warmed raspberries. The shrub is tall and erect and flowers only once. The loosely double flowers are quite large and are borne profusely enough to make a striking display. From a distance they appear to be tangerine orange. Closer inspection shows a glowing yellow base color with an overlay of shrimp pink and margins of deep copper. The reverse is tawny yellow.

## Rosa Alba

By some authorities **Rosa alba** is considered a hybrid, perhaps a natural one, between *R. damascena* and a white-flowered form of *R. canina*. It was grown in ancient Greece and Rome and was well known in Italy at the beginning of the fourteenth century when it was recommended as a hedge—and so it appears in early religious paintings where the Madonna is seated in a garden enclosed by intertwined branches of *R. alba*.

It is an exceptionally durable plant, free of disease,

thriving on neglect and in situations usually considered unsuitable for roses. Parkinson said of *Rosa Anglica alba*, as he termed it, that it "riseth up in some shadowie places, unto eight or ten foote high, with a stock of a great bignesse for a Rose." As a fact, a woody trunk "of great bignesse," developed over the long life of the plant, has earned it the folk name of Tree Rose.

Gerard described the White Rose as having "small leaves somwhat snipt about the edges, somwhat rough and of an overworne greene colour." Gerard's observation about the "somwhat snipt leaves" is astute: *R. alba*'s leaves are distinctive in having quite fine single teeth, not the doubly serrate margins of most roses. However, the "overworne greene colour" is hardly just, as the soft gray-green or blue-green leaves are a perfect setting for the delicately tinted flowers. The other botanical clue is that the receptacle is bowl-shaped or broadly ovoid, slightly indented at the top and supposedly furnished with glands and bristles only on the lower half. This is a reliable mark of identity when present, but all too often the hybrid nature of the plant asserts itself and the receptacle is either bare or entirely covered with bristles.

Having reached perfection in a small range of color, *Rosa alba* evidently felt no need to experiment further: its flowers are white, blush or clear mid-pink with no taint of magenta. The fully double forms are beautifully quartered, which makes one wonder whether 'Mme. Hardy' may have inherited her matchless form from an *alba* parent rather than from *R. centifolia* as Mr. Thomas suggests.

*Rosa alba semi-plena* must be an ancient garden form and not a true species as its name implies: it varies in the number of rows of petals when grown from seed, some being little more than single, others quite generously

filled. The specimens at the BBG are tall erect plants
with healthy blue-green foliage, never dull or rusty
though somewhat scanty at the base. The flowers are
borne in corymbs of six to eight and are at their most
charming when the center one opens within a ring of
taller buds. Newly opened flowers are faintly flushed
with pink, again recalling 'Mme. Hardy' and suggesting
kinship. The petals have a silky finish and are arranged
neatly around a central gold boss with an effect of wide-
eyed simplicity that calls to mind the word "innocence."
A severe critic might complain that the two-inch flowers
are too small in scale for the towering bush, but no harsh
judgment could withstand a breath of the delicious *alba*
scent. It is neither strong nor pervasive—you must approach closely to sniff it—but it is the distillation of pure
rose fragrance, never heavy or "stuffing," in the old term,
without any undertones of fruit or wine or musk but simply the quintessence of rose sweetness.

A more double form of this rose, *R. alba maxima*, had
been the emblem of the House of Lancaster for half a
century before the outbreak of the Wars of the Roses.
Shakespeare's dramatic depiction of the choice of red or
white roses in the Temple Garden is possibly more effective theater than authentic history.

**Maiden's Blush** is a treasured rose whose appearance
in medieval paintings proves its existence before the beginning of the fifteenth century. Because of the tough
constitution which is a valued family trait, it endures in
many abandoned gardens, marking the foundations of
vanished houses as lilacs do in New England. Its flowers
are of good size, some measuring over 3 inches across,
and are of muddled form, lacking the formal quartering
of other *albas*. The young foliage is light green and
downy on the reverse. Canes are lax enough to benefit

from support as recommended for *R. damascena*. The bud is framed by long feathered sepals which flare outwards as it begins to open. The color is enchanting: the newly opened flower is pale clear pink, fading lighter on the edges as it matures but always retaining the lovely blush in the center. The English name is appropriate and eminently proper, but in France the rose was given some delicately salacious titles that parallel Fragonard's paintings of courtly seduction. One of the names was 'Cuisse de Nymphe' while a more deeply colored form was 'Cuisse de Nymphe Émue' or Thigh of Aroused Nymph. It would take an overactive erotic imagination to find any suggestion of wanton behavior in this modest flower of virginal coloring and purity of fragrance.

## Rosa Centifolia

**Rosa centifolia** has gathered many names, a sure indication of popularity. The Rose of a Hundred Leaves, the Holland Rose and the Rose des Peintres are wholly suitable. A folk name, the Cabbage Rose, is misleading: the open cup-shaped flower crammed with short petals looks more like a head of loose-leaf lettuce than a solid cabbage. Another title, that of Province Rose, should be avoided because it invites confusion with the Provins Rose, *Rosa gallica,* which comes legitimately by the name as the mainstay of the perfume industry centered in the town of Provins.

Gerard wrote of the Holland Rose that it "hath divers shoots . . . ful of sharpe prickles . . . the flours grow on the tops of the branches, in shape and colour like the damaske Rose, but greater and more double, insomuch that the yellow chives in the middle are hard to be seene; of a reasonable good smell, but not fully so sweet as the common damaske Rose. . . ."

Parkinson agreed with Gerard's assessment, though apparently the two were at odds with the popular appraisal. Parkinson writes of "the great double Damask Province or Holland Rose," "the sent whereof commeth neerest unto the damaske rose, but yet is short of it by much, howsoever many doe think it as good as the damask, and to that end I have known some Gentlewomen have caused all their damaske stocks to be grafted with province Roses, hoping to have as good water, and more store of them then of damask Roses; but in my opinion it is not of halfe so good a sent as the water of damaske Roses" and he adds rather testily, apparently aware of the futility of reasoning with gentlewomen, "let every one follow their own fancie."

Gerard's name of Holland Rose is apt: its varieties are the triumph of the late sixteenth and seventeenth century plant breeders in the Netherlands. The roses were depicted in all their voluptuous fullness by the great Dutch and Flemish masters of flower painting who luxuriated in the languorous pose of the nodding flowers, gave them an improbable satiny gloss as if illuminated from within and ornamented them with oversize dewdrops. They painted them alone and in mixed bouquets, often attended by butterflies, bees and caterpillars. Sometimes the glow of the flowers was accented by translucent fruits, often cherries or grapes, and sometimes by contrasting textures such as birds' nests, these latter accessories being heaped at the base of the container to help balance the visual weight of the massed flowers.

As a garden plant, *Rosa centifolia* varies in habit. Some sorts are compact and upright; others are lanky and weak stemmed. The tall ones can be trained against a pillar, or staked, or have their canes tied together two or three feet above ground so that they benefit by mutual support yet can fling out their gracefully arching tips without constraint. The leaves are drooping, soft-hairy on the underside and edged with coarse single teeth which sometimes have tiny tufts of hair at their base. The canes are armed both with wiry bristles and with harsher prickles which in fact seem to be enlarged bristles as they are nearly straight and scarcely dilated at the base, unlike more conventional rose prickles which are hooked like a scimitar and fixed to the cane by an expanded attachment.

The sepals of R. *centifolia* are a feature of great beauty and a welcome means of recognition: they are much longer than the bud, deeply slashed and feathered and often provided with a spoon-shaped lobe at the tip. Instead of reflexing along the stalk, the sepals of *centifolia* varieties spread horizontally beneath the flower, framing it in a pointed ruff of stiff green lace which seems to support the neatly cupped outer petals. The stalk of the flower and the long ornate sepals are thickly covered with glands. These are worth noting as, when greatly enlarged and branched, they become the moss that distinguishes the *centifolia* mutations known as Moss Roses.

†'Vierge de Cléry,' as it is usually catalogued, is a low-growing, sturdy, late-flowering *centifolia* with striking purplish canes. The top of the furled bud is quite deep red with a curious metallic sheen. Surprisingly, it opens to a nearly pure white flower, sometimes warmed with a faint tinge of pink, sometimes with an ivory cast. On first opening, the outer segments form a cup around a central mass of short, narrow, fluffy petaloids with a de-

lightful translucent quality. As the flower matures, it opens nearly flat and reveals—in superior forms—a charming feature of some old roses called a button eye. This is formed by a ring of short petals, doubled over and so tightly packed in the receptacle that they can't free their tips but remain incurved in a cushionlike ring around the center of the flower. This is a small detail but one to watch for as it gives a trim finish to a flower and a reward of pleasure to the discerning eye.

Graham Thomas states that the correct name for 'Vierge de Cléry' is 'Unique Blanche.' This seems appropriate as the red-painted lips of the flower are more worldly than virginal. In his *The Old Shrub Roses,* Mr. Thomas recounts the discovery of this novel white rose in 1775 in an English cottage garden where it caught the keen eye of Mr. Daniel Greenwood of Kensington Nursery. One version of the story says that the cottager moved the plant from its original site "near a hedge on the contiguous premises of a Dutch merchant." It is plausible that the merchant brought a common pink *centifolia* from Holland and that it produced a white sport in its new home in England. The unanswerable question is why a Dutch rose found growing in England was given a string of French names?

## Moss Roses

Considering the antiquity of *Rosa gallica* and *R. damascena,* the Moss Roses are fairly recent additions to gardens. The first one appeared in Holland at the end of the seventeenth century and must have struck its owner with dismay as the apparent outbreak of a new disease.

With a few exceptions, Moss Roses are sports of *R. centifolia*. After the Dutch breeders had done their utmost with *centifolia,* its flowers were so completely double that all external reproductive parts had turned to petals. Since it was therefore sterile, the only way it could vary was by mutation, and this it did with great freedom. The earliest Moss Roses were typical *centifolias* except for their moss, the result of proliferation of the glands that cover the flower stalk, receptacle and sepals. These glands exude a sticky substance with a strong scent, often more resinous than fragrant, which adheres to anything it touches. The pretty saying, "A flower leaves its perfume on the hand that bestows it," applies with special force to Moss Roses.

The first of the Moss Roses, **Rosa centifolia muscosa,** is sometimes dated 1696 and sometimes a few years later. Its long string of names is evidence of wide distribution and popular affection: 'Common Moss,' 'Mousseux Ancien' and 'Old Pink Moss' are just a few. It is still the best in proportion, the most evocative of period charm, despite what later breeders (working with a fertile single form) could add in the way of size and diversity of color. It is a typical *centifolia* in every way except for the exaggerated mossiness. The leaves are mid-green with coarse single teeth, borne on a big plant with somewhat lax canes. The flower is a luscious pink with a hint of mauve. It is cup-shaped on first opening, then gradually expands to reveal a suggestion of quartering and a button eye, sometimes perfect, sometimes interspersed with upright petals. The delicacy of the flower is enhanced by the rough-textured sepals that frame it. The fragrance is extraordinary: potent, languorous, compelling. If you in-

**Mousseux Ancien.** The lowest flower shows an incomplete button eye.

herited your great-grandmother's Moss Rose china, this is the variety to accompany it.

*Rosa centifolia cristata,* the 'Crested Moss' or 'Chapeau de Napoléon,' is not a typical Moss Rose. Instead of having every surface below the flower covered with moss, this variety shows an individual pattern: its moss is confined to a bristly band down the center of each sepal, an arrangement that suggests a horse's roached mane or the shell of a beechnut. It is believed to be a sort of experimental mutation, parallel to the conventional Moss Roses but not identical to them, and is the single instance of *centifolia's* inventiveness along this line.

The bush is tall and sturdy. The large, bright pink flowers are borne in tight clusters so that the central flower, always the first to open, is hedged by masses of green-bearded buds. If you look straight down on a bud, its triangular shape may suggest a three-cornered hat—or perhaps the cockade worn on it—which may be sufficient reason for an admirer of Napoleon to link it with his name. In case a romantic association increases your pleasure in a flower, the variety was reputedly discovered growing on a convent wall in Switzerland in 1820.

†**Eugénie Guinoisseau** was introduced in 1864 and is almost certainly a hybrid. The plant spreads by suckers into a large thicket of slender upright canes clothed to the ground with handsome shiny foliage. The suckering habit and the velvety dark coloring of the flowers suggest *Rosa gallica* blood. The opening bud is brilliant fuchsia which deepens to pansy purple, then to near-black dahlia purple and ends as soft lilac. The flowers are small but are produced in great profusion. Since all the various stages are on view at once, a plant in full bloom gives an arresting polychrome effect. There is a defect:

some of the flowers are imperfect, lacking a pie-shaped sector or in extreme cases, a whole side, as if half the flower had been sliced off vertically. These deformed flowers are not noticeable except when examined closely. If they give offense, they can be snipped off without materially lessening the display.

**Gloire des Mousseux** (1852) in bud promises to live up to its bragging name. The sepals are as long as donkeys' ears, projecting far beyond the bud and elaborately slashed. At least as it grows in the BBG, this is the sum of its merits. The flower is mauve pink, of congested form; it fades to a dirty gray. It is far too large and heavy for the plant, both aesthetically and physically, to the extent that one cane pulled off at the base under the burden of a single bloom.

**Comtesse de Murinais** (1843), a six-footer seen at the New York Botanical Garden, was so fervently admired that it will be planted in the BBG as soon as Tillotson's can fill the order. The foliage is handsome and dense, of a brighter green than is usual with Moss Roses. The sepals are short but well furnished with bright green moss which makes a rich setting for the pink-tinted buds. On opening, the blush tint soon fades but a hint of ivory remains, just enough to keep the flowers from being lifeless white. The flowers are of good size and well filled with broad petals of firm substance. Graham Thomas believes the variety shows Damask affinity. If so, this would partly account for the flowers' delicious, intensely strong, head-swiming fragrance.

**Salet** (1854) is quite a deep rose-pink fading to mauve. Sepals are short and nicely feathered on the margins but sparingly mossed. The flowers are irregular in form with broad guard petals enclosing a mass of narrow segments. 'Salet' is rare among Moss Roses in producing flowers throughout the season. The variety would be good for cutting because of its decisive color but its garden effect is diminished by tall new growth which overtops the flowers and conceals them.

**Mme. Louis Lévêque** is a Hybrid Moss introduced in 1898. Its mixed blood gives it the valuable habit of repeat flowering but with a loss of good proportion and period authenticity. Mr. Thomas thinks its non-Moss parent was a Hybrid Perpetual which would account for the oversized flower. The bud is outstandingly beautiful. As the long sepals part, they disclose tightly furled petals of delicate mauve pink with a translucent quality that resembles fine porcelain. However, the open flower— cupped, crammed with petals in an overstuffed way, and four inches or more across—looks ill at ease on a dainty Moss Rose plant. Compared to genuine unadulterated Moss Roses, 'Mme. Louis Lévêque' borders on the grotesque. Then as now, it is difficult for breeders to understand that you can't improve on perfection, that *bigger* isn't necessarily *better,* and that *hybrid* can also mean *mongrel.*

## THE BOURBON ROSES

Of all the classes of old roses, only the Bourbons have an impeccable pedigree. The first of its kind was a natural hybrid between the Pink Autumn Damask (Virgil's Rose of a Double Spring) and Parson's Pink China. It was discovered growing with its parents on the French island of Bourbon (now Réunion) east of Madagascar. Seed of the hybrid was sent to Paris where it produced a second generation of superior garden forms. These retained the rich fragrance of the Damask parent while the

China Rose contributed its precious gifts of repeat blooming and a unique silky translucent finish of the petals—and inevitably, in some of its descendants, a lack of hardiness.

Though the pure Bourbons are very full, their petals are so tissue-fine that they don't look congested. They are nearly spherical in form, with outer petals incurved like a cup which opens just enough to give a glimpse of imbricated petals, sometimes quartered, sometimes taking an orderly swirl that suggests the foliated tracery of a Gothic window. These are the costly silk roses that adorned French millinery and were the envy of children whose straw sailors were wreathed with common cornflowers, poppies and daisies. The Bourbon roses have an ethereal delicacy, a period quality so pervasive that it is difficult to understand how Victorian taste permitted them to be superseded by their stodgy, overstuffed offspring, the Hybrid Perpetuals.

By a wry and frustrating coincidence, the BBG had no Bourbons in its collection. Those planted in 1978 didn't flower in their first year. The New York Botanical Garden's inventory of old roses includes 'Variegata di Bologna' but, when sought out, its label marked a thicket of *R. multiflora* understock which had totally routed the named variety. Since the authors refuse to describe any rose they haven't grown or seen growing, they can do no more than refer wistful old-rose enthusiasts to the seductive portraits in Tillotson's catalogues and in *The Old Shrub Roses* and beg them to wait, as we must do, for the newly planted Bourbons, and those on order, to come into bloom.

In order not to leave the Bourbon scoreboard a complete blank, we can mention **Ferdinand Pichard** (1921) usually listed as a Hybrid Perpetual but classed as a

Ferdinand Pichard.

Bourbon in Britain. It is a mid-sized flower, cup-shaped, not overly full, with a base color of soft pink ornamented with bold stripes, feathering, stippling or sometimes a whole petal of deeper rose or crimson. The contrast between base color and variegation is not so sharp as the photograph renders it: allowance must be made for the tendency of film to exaggerate the density of red tones. 'Ferdinand Pichard' is not a gaudy flower but a pleasing oddity that is enhanced by delightful perfume. It is advertised as repeat blooming but flowers only once in the BBG.

Tillotson's 1978 catalogue lists seven Bourbons, though for our climate, the reputedly tender 'Souvenir de la Malmaison' should be deducted. In exchange, 'Reine des Violettes' (1860) can be added as it is closer to the cupped, nearly spherical Bourbon form than to the Hybrid Perpetuals where it is usually found. The knowledge that some of these treasures are in the BBG shrub rose borders gives added reason to long for June.

## HYBRID PERPETUALS

Hybrid Perpetuals are derived chiefly from the Bourbon Rose with admixtures of other hybrids, especially those of the repeat-flowering China Rose. Despite this reinforced infusion of China blood, only a few of the HPs justify their name by flowering more than once. 'Frau Karl Druschki,' described on page 63, is an exception. The color range is limited: white through various rose-pinks to crimson, carmine and magenta. Many of them fade badly; few last well in water. The flowers are obese, short necked and dull in finish. The BBG grows nine varieties. Few visitors notice them.

There's a saying that your grandmother's furniture and jewelry are antiques; your mother's, merely old-fashioned. This aptly applies to HPs which are not old enough to have period value and not new enough to compete with modern roses. Judging from the lack of interest shown by visitors to the BBG, it appears that most gardeners would be disappointed with them. Their chief merit in contemporary gardens is their intense fragrance, a grace that is largely lost in modern roses through breeders' exclusive concentration on achieving new colors.

Nevertheless the Brownstone Revival has sparked renewed interest in Victoriana and it may be, as the tide of fashion turns with a new generation, that Hybrid Perpetuals will come back into favor. For the record, then, it may be of value to list the varieties growing in the BBG and the New York Botanical Garden (NYBG from now on) so that nurserymen will know where to find budwood of varieties not listed by Tillotson's. Prospective buyers can view the roses and make their own comparisons.

## PINK HYBRID PERPETUALS

**Heinrich Munch** (1911—NYBG) heads the list. It is a relatively small bush with tremendous blooms of a lovely clear pink, quite luminous and untainted with magenta, all borne on one level for maximum effect. It is a repeat bloomer and intensely fragrant.

**American Beauty** (1875—NYBG) has low-arching canes with huge, fat, short-stemmed flowers at each node. The color is Persian rose or shocking pink or the most uninhibited cerise you can put a name to, with a curious smoky overtone that keeps it from shouting the house down. A group of three plants, set close enough so that their lax canes could overlap to make a solid mound, would be smashingly effective.

**Baroness Rothschild** (1868) and **Baronne Prevost** (1839) are both grown at the NYBG. They are rose-pink, not especially remarkable and not equal in clarity to 'Heinrich Munch.'

### CARMINE AND MAGENTA HYBRID PERPETUALS

**Captain Hayward** (1893—BBG) is a showy plant with a spectacular display of magenta blooms that almost blanket the plant. It is supposedly remontant but blooms only once at the BBG.

**Fisher Holmes** (1865—BBG) is an unusually shapely plant with dense foliage. The flowers, crimson fading badly to magenta, are powerfully fragrant.

**Ulrich Brunner** (1881—BBG) like 'Fisher Holmes,' starts out carmine red but fades distressingly. The fragrance is superb.

### RED HYBRID PERPETUALS

There are two deep red Hybrid Perpetuals with white edges, so remarkably ugly that it is hard to understand how they have remained in cultivation. **Roger Lambelin** (1890—BBG) is a scant-petaled flower of deep crimson with irregularly twisted petals whose outer edges are snipped into points and edged with a thin line of white. Some of the petals have a chalky smudge down the center. The effect is of a badly distressed flower, misshapen and bug-bitten around the margin. **Baron Girod de l'Ain** (1897—NYBG) is a somewhat brighter red than 'Roger Lambelin' and has less conspicuous white edges, thus is somewhat easier to look at.

**Général Jacqueminot** (1852—BBG) has more value today as an historical milestone in rose breeding than as a garden ornament. It is a descendant of an innovative early Bourbon, 'Gloire des Rosomanes' (1825), which combined a rich crimson color, repeat blooming, vigorous growth and Damask fragrance. For many years, 'Général Jacqueminot' was the apex of achievement, the criterion by which other red roses were rated. Extensively used in breeding, it became the progenitor of a distinguished list of Hybrid Perpetuals. As recently as 1931, it produced 'Soeur Thérèse' which, when mated with 'Crimson Glory,' brought forth 'Charlotte Armstrong,' a prolific matron with a proud roster of notable offspring. It is likely that the Général's blood is still operative in fragrant, full-petaled red roses such as 'Mister Lincoln.'

'Général Jacqueminot' grows in the east shrub border of the BBG. If you walk past the second double arch, look for the Général between the climber 'The Beacon' and the lattice fence. The Général's fully double flowers open deep crimson and fade to reddish purple. The heavy flowers sometimes nod, a tendency to weak necks which is perhaps inherited from the Bourbon ancestor. Newly opened flowers have a dark velvety bloom which is one of the Général's most valued legacies to its offspring. Its intense fragrance, however, has been diluted in successive generations. One deep sniff of an open bloom of 'Général Jacqueminot' will tell you what modern roses have lost.

# 7
# Shrub Roses and Climbers

How big is a shrub rose? You may as well ask, "How big is a dog?" The class is extremely elastic, comprising many combinations of bloodlines and some strays that don't fit anywhere else. No description can be devised to cover all variations, but as a tentative guide, the plants are larger than those of Hybrid Teas while their flowers are smaller, less double and less formal in shape.

## ROSA RUGOSA

*Rosa rugosa* and its hybrids are certainly the most valuable group of shrub roses. This stalwart Oriental is the rose you see flourishing in nearly pure sand within reach of salt spray at bathing beaches and shorefront cottages. It is hardy to −50°F, that is, to the tree line in northern Canada. Its intensely fragrant flowers, remontant in many varieties, are followed by large colorful hips which are both decorative and useful for preserves. The rough-surfaced leaves from which the species takes its name are typically dark green, crinkled and leathery, immune to disease, and too tough to be palatable to insects—though Japanese beetles will devour the open flowers. Rugosa roses are in short the perfect selection for the gardener who wants roses but hasn't the time or inclination to fuss with them.

The type is single or semidouble, mostly crimson but sometimes deep rose or, less often, white. The flowers are short stemmed and apt to be hidden by vigorous leafy growth. However, the delicious scent is powerfully apparent even when the flowers are partly concealed.

Two semidouble white forms are in commerce. Neither can be recommended as a garden plant. Both **Blanc Double de Coubert** and *Rosa rugosa albo-plena* have the damning fault of not being self-cleaning: the petals of spent flowers, limp and brown, hang on like scraps of wet grocery bags. They are so unsightly that they cancel the modest appeal of the irregularly formed flowers. It's a no-win situation: if you take time each day to cut off the offending dead blossoms, you sacrifice the hips which are one of the great attractions of Rugosas.

It is sometimes felt that species roses should keep their natural simplicity and not be tampered with by breeders. In the case of the Rugosas, some of the hybrids are a great improvement on the type, combining the vitality, health and rich fragrance of the wild parent with the clear colors of modern roses. Few of the Rugosas now growing in the BBG are available in commerce. However, with the resurgence of interest in shrub roses, it may be well to note the most desirable ones in case they reappear in catalogues. Conversely, the dowdy or downright ugly ones can be avoided with advance warning.

**Dr. Eckener** (1930) is one of the most delightful of Rugosa hybrids. Its non-Rugosa parent was a long-forgotten Hybrid Tea called 'Golden Emblem' which gave 'Dr. Eckener' its deep yellow base color while the Rugosa contributed bright salmon-rose on the outer half of the petals. The grainy gold stamens characteristic of Rugosa roses add to its charm. 'Dr. Eckener' is a tall plant: if allowed to grow naturally, its delectable flowers may be carried too high for easy enjoyment of its singular fragrance and radiant color. It is at its best when trained horizontally along a fence where it will flower at every node, forming a garland whose scent will make your head swim when you lean over it. Its rescue from oblivion may be worth recounting as it exemplifies the constant plight of endangered roses and the need for active preservation.

The plant in the picture was bought from Bobbink & Atkins (of honored memory) in 1941. It was too large to consider digging when the owners moved to another state in 1958. However, the gardener was determined to have 'Dr. Eckener' as backdrop for a new rose garden. Budwood was sent to Joseph Kern for propagation; a new plant returned in due time. Mr. Kern carried 'Dr. Eckener' for many years. When it was learned that he was about to retire, the BBG ordered 'Dr. Eckener' just in the nick of time, obtaining the very last plants Mr. Kern had in his fields. From these plants budwood was sent to Tillotson's early in 1978, so this enchanting variety will once more be available to gardeners.

In retrospect, it is unfortunate that 'Dr. Eckener's' sport **Golden King** (1935) wasn't similarly preserved. It was trained on wires below and at the sides of two windows where its luminous primrose-yellow flowers glowed with enhanced radiance against rose-red bricks

**Dr. Eckener.** The effort required to train a shrub rose horizontally on a fence is repaid by profusion of bloom.

while its delicious scent flowed into the room. Inquiries to the present owner of the house have brought no reply so it appears that this meltingly lovely rose has been lost. If anyone knows of a source or has a plant from which they'd be willing to contribute budwood, please hasten the information to the BBG. Since all our rarities are

**Golden King.** Does this lost beauty still exist?

shared with Tillotson's, avid gardeners will know our search has been a success if they find 'Golden King' listed in some future catalogue.

**Agnes** (*Rosa rugosa* x *R. foetida persiana,* 1922) is much inferior to 'Golden King' but is, ironically, available in commerce. Its flowers are poorly formed, with loose shaggy petals upstanding in a rather disheveled way. The attractive coppery buds quickly open to pale straw yellow blooms, a retreating color with little garden effect though with the typical Rugosa perfume. While it is described as being sparingly remontant, 'Agnes' produces no flowers in the BBG after its blooming period in early June.

**Pink Grootendorst** (a sport of 'F. J. Grootendorst,' 1923) is a charmer. Its tight clusters of rose-pink flowers, lightly touched with salmon, have snipped edges like tiny carnations, an appealing eccentricity no doubt inherited from its Polyantha ancestor. The sturdy bush is well clothed to the ground with light green, strongly ribbed leaves. The flower clusters, set among the leaves on short stems, make a prodigious display in early summer and persist until killing frost, not so lavishly as in their first appearance, but still generously enough to make a telling show of color. Unlike the great majority of their tribe, the flowers are scentless, the only demerit to mark against this attractive hybrid. Budwood of 'Pink Grootendorst' was sent to Tillotson's in 1978, so it will be available in the near future.

**Grootendorst Supreme** (1936), like 'Pink Grootendorst,' is a sport of 'F. J. Grootendorst' (1918), which is a hybrid of *Rosa rugosa* and an unknown Polyantha. The flowers of 'Grootendorst Supreme' are a retreating shade of dull russet red with none of the sparkle of the pink form and—in the BBG at least—few if any flowers after its initial bloom in early summer.

**Max Graf** (1919) is a creeper, not strictly a shrub rose, but may be admitted here because of the Rugosa blood that endowed it with fair-sized, lively salmon-pink single flowers. From its other parent, *Rosa wichuraiana,* it derives its glossy foliage and semiprostrate habit. 'Max Graf' is the rose that covers the bank leading up to the latticed pavilion in the BBG rose garden. It is strange that this hardy, versatile, cheerful little plant has been dropped from growers' lists as it makes an admirable ground cover and, when judiciously placed, is guaranteed to keep the newsboy from taking short cuts across your lawn.

**Ruskin** (1928) is one of the hybrids that seem embarrassed by their mixed blood. It is a child of a bright red Hybrid Rugosa, 'Souvenir de Pierre Leperdieux' (1895) and 'Victor Hugo' (1884), a globular crimson-purple

**Pink Grootendorst.** The derivation of this hybrid is clearly indicated by its carnationlike Polyantha flowers and crinkled, heavy-textured Rugosa foliage.

Hybrid Perpetual. The resulting velvety crimson, fully double HP flowers look incongrous against a background of crinkled Rugosa foliage. If you have ever seen foundation plantings decorated for Christmas with plastic poinsettias wired to the terminal rosettes of rhododendrons, you will know exactly the feeling of uneasiness that 'Ruskin' arouses. The flowers are unfading—a substantial virtue in red roses—but some are malformed and buds may ball in wet weather. When perfectly formed flowers are half open, they have a good spiral center but quickly spread to show their golden center. Even with its acknowledged faults, 'Ruskin' would be welcome as a deep red, richly fragrant rose in areas where winters are too severe for Hybrid Teas.

**Amélie Gravereaux** (['Général Jacqueminot' x 'Maréchal Niel'] x 'Conrad Ferdinand Meyer,' 1903) has quite exceptional ancestry. 'Général Jacqueminot' is the splendid red Hybrid Perpetual whose name has been cited many times through its influence in the breeding of Hybrid Teas. 'Maréchal Niel' (1864) is a famous yellow climber, highly esteemed in warm climates but not seen in northern gardens because of its tenderness. This may explain why 'Maréchal Niel' has been used so seldom as a parent: in fact, this is the first time its name has been noted as a participant in the breeding of this century's garden roses. It is difficult to guess what the Maréchal contributed to this curious mélange unless it is the oddly pale color of the leaves. However, it seems certain that the Maréchal's lack of hardiness was countered by the influence of 'Conrad Ferdinand Meyer,' a rather dingy light pink Hybrid Rugosa. There can be no doubt that 'Général Jacqueminot's' potent blood determined the color of 'Amélie Gravereaux,' whose well-shaped flowers, cupped on first opening, are rich crimson fading to

Tyrian rose, with a satiny sheen and powerful fragrance. The leaves are less crinkled and much lighter green than is typical of Rugosas: they make a strongly contrasting background for the radiant flowers. After the burst of June bloom, the plant produces a spattering of flowers during the rest of the season, never many at a time but enough to make a modest showing and provide a breath of intense sweetness.

**Amélie Gravereaux.**

**Vanguard** (1932) is given a questionable pedigree. It is described as being a hybrid of *Rosa wichuraiana* and *R. rugosa alba*. Since these are both white roses, it seems unlikely that they could have produced a child with·brilliant orange-salmon flowers. 'Vanguard' is described as having large double flowers on strong stems. This is a variety the BBG would very much like to add to its collection. If anyone knows a source or has budwood to contribute, please let us know.

The precarious plight of old roses should be amply demonstrated by the many examples of endangered varieties named in this and the previous chapter. It is hoped that lovers of old roses will rally to provide the BBG or other botanic gardens with stock so that no more eminently desirable roses will follow 'Golden King' into what is feared may be extinction.

With many first-rate varieties to choose from, it would be folly to waste garden space on those with marked defects. Readers who are fortunate enough to live near the BBG can study these unrecommended roses and judge for themselves whether the following assessments are just. If you find these varieties listed, you will be warned to have second thoughts about ordering them.

**Conrad Ferdinand Meyer** (1899) has poorly formed, veiny, light rose-pink flowers with a disagreeably pungent, nose-prickling scent rather like that of boiling vinegar.

**Nova Zembla** (1907) has flowers of very pale gray-pink fading to oyster white, so deficient in brilliance that they fortunately escape notice. The plant is leggy, with sparse canes of angular form.

**Roseraie de l'Hay** (1901). Field notes read "horrid crumpled magenta" with no extenuating detail.

**Hansa** (1905) is a bare-shanked plant with flowers of grayed magnolia purple fading to muted mauve. The petals are sometimes streaked with lighter color but this minor note of individuality is not enough to relieve the general dinginess.

**Sir Thomas Lipton** (1900). If you enter the BBG rose garden by the west gate and turn left, you will find this rose third on the left, behind the first pillar rose. According to old Bobbink & Atkins catalogues, the variety should be white—specifically "snowy white," to leave no possible uncertainty—whereas the one in the BBG is a rather washed-out light pink. Since *Rosa rugosa alboplena* and 'Blanc Double de Coubert' both fail in elementary hygiene, it would be very desirable to have a pure white double Rugosa, always providing that it is self-cleaning. If anyone has stock of the true 'Sir Thomas Lipton,' please send us word.

## ROSA SPINOSISSIMA

As its name indicates, **Rosa spinosissima** is the prickliest possible: its canes are densely armed with sharp bristles and prickles. Common names for the species include Scotch rose and Burnet rose, the latter noting the resemblance of the dainty, finely toothed foliage to that of the cucumber-flavored salad burnet, *Sanguisorba minor*. These are rugged shrubs, rarely exceeding four feet in their wild forms and hardy to −20°F. Since they are admirably adapted to form hedges of moderate height and width, it is regrettable that so few are now in commerce, especially when rampantly invasive weeds like *Rosa multiflora* are widely advertised for the purpose. It's true that most Scotch roses flower only once but since this habit doesn't diminish the popularity of shrubs such as forsythia and mock orange, there's little reason why it should prejudice growers against the Scotch roses.

One in particular should be noted in case it ever becomes available. (If it still exists, will you tell us at the BBG?) It is *Rosa spinosissima altaica,* a sturdy but graceful shrub whose branches arch to sweep the ground. The fountainlike canes bear a double row of 3-inch creamy yellow single flowers, each with a lavish brush of yellow stamens, starting in mid-May. The fragrance is still fresh in memory after twenty-odd years: a rich old-rose scent overlaid with that of warm boiled custard at the instant vanilla is added. The mingled odors are not fully perceived at close range but are best enjoyed when the perfume drifts through the garden, forming pools of scent on warm windless days. As you pass through these concentrations of scent, so strong and so teasing, you will find yourself sniffing nearby flowers until the Scotch rose catches your eye and recalls the source. Francis Bacon, in his often-quoted essay "Of Gardens," praised flowers that liberally release their perfume on the air "where it comes and goes, like the warbling of music." One wonders what Bacon would have said about floating vanilla custard?

Two hybrids of *R. spinosissima* are still in cultivation: 'Harison's Yellow' and 'Stanwell Perpetual.' The first is thought to be a cross between the Scotch rose and *R. foetida persiana* from which the hybrid takes its bright yellow color. The bush is tall and immensely vigorous, and is furnished with rich bright green leaves which make a perfect setting for the semidouble, sweetly scented, sunny yellow flowers.

**Harison's Yellow** was bred either by Richard Harison or his son, George Folliott Harison, and was introduced in 1830, a year after the death of the father at the age of

*Rosa spinosissima altaica.*

82. It is uncertain whether the aging man or his son, an equally keen plantsman, did the actual hybridizing. No matter which Harison is credited with the birth of their namesake, its place of origin will bring a little glow of chauvinistic pride to New York City dwellers: the rose first bloomed at the Harisons' country estate which oc-

cupied what is now the block between 30th and 31st Streets and 8th and 9th Avenues.

**Stanwell Perpetual** is a cross between a Scotch rose and the Autumn Damask, *R. damascena bifera*. It is a charming plant, about five feet tall, with the arching grace of the Scotch rose and even tinier gray-green leaflets. The cameo-pink flowers are the size of a silver dollar and open flat, sometimes as irregular doubles but often showing perfect button eyes. The plant starts to flower very early in the season and is still producing flowers and buds when frost ends its display in late November. Everblooming roses were a rarity in 1838 when 'Stanwell Perpetual' was introduced. If it had not been sterile, it would undoubtedly have had a decisive role in rose breeding. Francis Bacon would have classed 'Stanwell Perpetual' among "fast flowers of their scent," that is, chary of dispersing their fragrance. It is in fact so little pervasive that you would think it lacked scent if you merely walk by the bush. You have to put your nose to a blossom to catch its light, pure, honeylike perfume—and when you discover it, you'll return again and again. It is not a showy rose by any means. Its delicate appeal is evident only on close examination, but if you have an eye for miniature perfection, you will find a place for 'Stanwell Perpetual' in your shrub border and in your choicest small vases.

**Frühlingsgold** (1937) is a more recent hybrid Scotch rose. It is a cross between the sulphur-yellow *R. spinosissima hispida* and 'Joanna Hill,' a peaches-and-cream Hybrid Tea introduced in 1928. 'Joanna Hill' is no longer listed by dealers in garden roses but is still grown for the cut-flower trade. More important, it lives in its progeny which, in addition to 'Frühlingsgold,' include 'Eclipse' and 'Peace.' 'Joanna Hill' was noted for its

**Stanwell Perpetual.** The flowers show perfect button eyes.

elegant pointed buds, deep yellow marked with ribbons of carmine between the parting sepals. This trait is inherited by 'Frühlingsgold' and adds to its attraction. 'Frühlingsgold' is an enormously vigorous, iron-hardy shrub growing 10 to 12 feet tall. Its lower canes are stiffly erect but arch outwards at the top to display very large semidouble flowers of a luscious shade of mid-yellow softening to cream, with a conspicuous central brush of deep gold stamens. In cool springs, the underside of the petals carries a subtle suffusion of pink. The flowers scent the air for yards around: they are always boiling with bees which apparently find the perfume as seductive as do humans. Because of its stature,

'Frühlingsgold' must either be pruned hard to keep its flowers at eye and nose level, or trained on a fence like 'Dr. Eckener' as described on page 197. The mature canes are enormously thick and woody but the young shoots, while still succulent and malleable, might accept the discipline of horizontal training.

'Frühlingsgold' is no longer in commerce though Mrs. Wiley of Tillotson's keeps a plant in her display garden. She would very likely bud plants on special order for those who have fallen in love with the variety at the BBG where its powerful fragrance outweighs that of the wisteria that flowers at the same time.

*Rosa hugonis* belongs to the same subgenus as *R. spinosissima:* its strong family resemblance may justify including it in a discussion of that species. *R. hugonis* has much the same broad arching habit as 'Stanwell Perpetual,' with a mist of tiny bright green leaflets as delicate as maidenhair fronds reduced to miniature size. Its single yellow flowers, no larger than two inches across but closely set on the graceful canes, have a light clover-like fragrance. As the first rose to open, usually a day or two before the middle of May, they serve as a welcome herald for impatient gardeners who start looking for spring the day after Christmas. *Rosa hugonis* was discovered in western China by a Catholic missionary, Father Hugh Scannon, who collected seed and sent it to Kew in 1899. Although it has great charm as a garden plant and considerable interest as representing a rare color in wild roses, *Rosa hugonis* seems to have had no significant role in rose breeding. It is likely that rose fanciers of the day were dazzled by the appearance of 'Soleil d'Or,' a showy double with occasional recurrent bloom, and had no incentive to start from scratch with a single-flowered, short-season species.

## ROSA FOETIDA

*Rosa foetida,* its double variety *R. f. persiana* and the brilliantly colored *R. f. bicolor* have been frequently cited as the source of the intense yellow and orange tones in modern roses. Neither the type nor *bicolor* does well in the BBG: they must be replaced every year or two. You may observe small weak specimens just south of the west gate if indeed they are still alive. It is unfortunate that these seminal roses are so intractable, as an opportunity to examine the plants would increase appreciation of the skill of the breeders who elaborated this century's roses from these simple beginnings.

## HYBRID MUSK

**Will Scarlet** (1950) is the best large everblooming shrub rose in the BBG. It stands a good eight feet tall, well clothed to the base and dense enough to make an impenetrable hedge or screen to shut out an undesirable view. It is restrained in spread, unlike the rampaging *Rosa multiflora* which turns your property into an instant blackberry patch. The canes are stout and erect: from them the flowering shoots spray outwards from the top nearly to the base. The major period of bloom is in early summer but after this spectacular effort the plant provides a continuous supply of flowers, enough to make a strong statement of color. The semidouble 2½ inch flowers, borne in showy clusters of 15 to 18, are of a curious shade of light crimson tending to rose madder in some lights yet with a faint shadowy overtone of russet or brown. Their scent is neither strong nor roselike yet not unpleasant: it suggests a pair of new pigskin gloves.

## Climbing Roses

Before you invest in climbing roses, you should be advised that what counts is not the initial cost but the upkeep. When you start with a new plant, you tie up the canes to whatever support you have provided. The next year you do the same, fastening the new canes over the older ones. With each year's additions, the accumulation of aging, dead or unproductive wood gets more deeply buried and more difficult to remove, as ultimately it must. If your rose is growing on a freestanding trellis or arbor, you can reach in from the back, cut the canes into sections and drag them piecemeal through the thorny thickets, with some expense of blood and blasphemy. The other method, and one that is necessary if your rose is trained to a house wall, is to cut all the fastenings and pull the entire mass of canes free of their support. In the case of a long-established heavy-wooded rose, it is wise to lean the canes against a stepladder to keep them semierect rather than risk bruised or broken canes if they are bent sharply to lie on the ground. It is then fairly easy to cut out all the old wood before tying the young canes back into position. The same rejuvenation must be performed on roses trained to a fence, but this is considerably easier as the canes are at waist level instead of over your head.

The large number of climbers, both historical and recent, represented at the BBG makes it impossible to allot them horizontal growing room. Instead they are trained straight up the boundary fences with a saving of space but with some loss in the quantity of bloom. Since they are sharply pruned every year, the buildup of old canes is no problem. However, the heavy-wooded 'Silver Moon' which covers the north side of the west gateway and flings itself over the top is given its way until some crisis occurs—painting time for the trellis or replacement of posts or beams—when the aged canes with their razor-sharp prickles must be disentangled from the lattice, an operation only slightly less lacerating to the arms than trying to manicure a tiger.

**Silver Moon** (1910) is the climber to choose if you want to slipcover a barn with roses. It is a prodigious grower with handsome foliage and enormous saucer-shaped single flowers, white with a creamy tinge on first opening and with a generous brush of gold stamens to enhance their purity. The plant at the west gate dates from the beginning of the rose garden in 1927. Its age is attested to by the size of the gnarled woody burl from which the canes spring: it measures 27 inches across. The pedigree of 'Silver Moon' is uncertain. It is tentatively given as (*Rosa wichuraiana* x 'Devoniensis') x *R. laevigata*. Taking the parents in reverse order, *R. laevigata* is the Cherokee Rose, a 20-foot climber with highly polished foliage and fragrant single flowers in pink, white or red. It is so widely naturalized in the South that most people assume it is a native and are surprised to learn that it originated in China. *R. wichuraiana* is also an Oriental. It is a low-arching plant with limber canes, shiny light green foliage and pyramids of small single white flowers. 'Devoniensis,' despite its specific-sounding name, is an ancient Tea Rose dating to 1838, described as having creamy-white petals and sweet fragrance. It is probable that *wichuraiana*'s −10°F hardiness counteracted *laevigata*'s intolerance of frost while *laevigata* added height and stiffness to *wichuraiana*'s lax canes. Since 'Devoniensis' is known only as a printed description, it is not possible to guess what it contributed to 'Silver Moon' unless it is a trace of fragrance and the cream-to-ivory tint that infuses the climber's whiteness with warmth.

**City of York** ('Prof. Gnau' x 'Dorothy Perkins,' 1945) is a delightful white climber of more manageable scale than 'Silver Moon.' The flowers are creamy white with a pleasing flush of yellow in the depths and a marked fragrance, an unusual grace in climbers. On first opening, the outer petals form a collar while the center stays neatly rounded. As each flower matures, it opens flat to show a rich gold heart. 'City of York' occasionally offers a scattering of flowers in summer, a trait it inherits—with all its good points—from its fragrant, cream-white Hybrid Tea parent, 'Prof. Gnau.' It takes its moderate climbing habit from the well-known pink Rambler, 'Dorothy Perkins,' but happily not the Rambler's excessive susceptibility to mildew.

**New Dawn** (1930) is a sport of 'Dr. W. Van Fleet' (1910). An early Bobbink & Atkins catalogue hailed 'New Dawn' as "The first hardy everblooming Climber." If their claim is correct, then 'New Dawn' deserves its place in the BBG among historic roses. It is worth noting that one of 'Dr. W. Van Fleet's' grandparents was *Rosa wichuraiana,* a species that appears in the pedigree of the best climbing roses as often as 'Crimson Glory' and 'Eva' do in the bloodlines of Hybrid Teas and Floribundas. 'New Dawn' is a very pale uniform blush pink. The buds are charmingly long-pointed and firm but open too quickly into somewhat loosely formed flowers. These are borne on stems long enough for cutting. Like those of 'Gay Princess,' the flowers of 'New Dawn' look especially attractive in a silver container. Gardeners have become so accustomed to the lively yellow tints at the base of more recent pink roses, beginning with 'Pinocchio' and moving on to 'Confidence,' 'Sierra Dawn' and 'Pristine,' that an unrelieved pale pink rose appears to lack sparkle. In spite of strong growth, healthy foliage and repeat blooming, a candid critic must state that 'New Dawn' is insipid.

**America** (AARS 1976) looks highly desirable in its catalogue portrait, with flowers of radiant coral rose. Unfortunately our acquaintance with the variety ends there. The plants we received were so weak that all but one of them died. The survivor is barely a foot tall with toothpick canes: it is unlikely to show life next spring. We mean to try again.

As with Hybrid Teas, there are a great number of red climbers in the market. **Dr. Huey** ('Ethel' x 'Gruss an Teplitz,' 1920) should be mentioned not so much for its attractions, which are minimal, but so you will be warned to recognize it if it appears at the base of one of your cherished rosebushes. 'Dr. Huey' is sometimes used as understock on which other roses are budded. While it is no more apt to put out suckers than is *Rosa multiflora*, it is more insidious because its leaves are indistinguishable from those of HTs or Floribundas. It may suffocate a more desirable plant before its flowers proclaim it an impostor. The semidouble ruffled flowers are very dark maroon made slightly more visible by a ring of white at the base of the petals. 'Dr. Huey,' with only one short period of bloom, has no claim to garden space either on a trellis or at the root of one of your rosebushes.

**Blaze** ('Paul's Scarlet Climber' x 'Gruss an Teplitz,' 1932) is a much overused variety whose shapeless flowers open crimson and turn magenta, a jarring discord in blossoms closely massed in a cluster.

**Cadenza** ('New Dawn' x 'Cl. Embers,' 1967) has 'Floradora,' a grandchild of 'Eva,' as grandparent on one side, the only instance we've come across of a descendant of one of the patriarchs lending its proud inheritance to a climber. 'Cadenza' has splendid stout canes and clean foliage. The urn-shaped buds open to well-filled flowers of deep blood red which hold their color without fading or bluing until the petals drop. They have a slight but agreeable fragrance combining a hint of old rose with a strong dash of tea. 'Cadenza' is truly everblooming: it still showed a few flowers and buds when frost lowered the curtain in late November.

**Tempo** ('Climbing Ena Harkness' x unnamed seedling, 1975) is something of a puzzle. Advertised as a climber, the longest cane it produced in two years was 43 inches. The lovely spiral buds are purest blood red. They open to flat flowers of rose-red, some with weak necks. The perfume is uncommonly strong and pleasing. 'Tempo' may not be the red climber we have looked for but it is a very positive step on the way to breeding one.

**Don Juan** ('New Dawn' seedling x 'New Yorker,' 1958) is the best red climber in the BBG, deserving more critical acclaim than it has received. Though unrelated, it might be a twin of the HT 'Scarlet Knight.' They are so much alike that the photograph of 'Scarlet Knight' on page 24 will serve for either one. The flowers of 'Don Juan' are perfectly flat: their rippled, imbricated petals are brilliant currant red with a velvety black-maroon bloom in the shadows. Most of the blooms are borne singly on long stems. They have a moderate scent, no doubt inherited from their HT parent, the intensely fragrant 'New Yorker.' 'Don Juan' continues to bloom throughout the summer—never a great profusion but a dependable display—and is only halted by killing frost.

Yellow climbers are few but cherished. **Golden Showers** ('Charlotte Armstrong' x 'Captain Thomas,' AARS 1957) has beautiful pointed buds of burnt orange, opening to canary-yellow flowers which may measure as

**Elegance's** exuberant growth makes it an admirable enclosure for a rose garden.

much as 5¾ inches across. Red filaments, such as are found in single roses and a few semidoubles such as 'Ivory Fashion,' accentuate the charm of the open flower. Unfortunately, as they age they fade to ivory and go limp, and though the petals eventually fall of their own accord, they hang on for a depressingly long time, detracting from the sunny freshness of the younger flowers. 'Golden Showers' repeats sparingly, but can't truly be termed everblooming as is the case with 'Cadenza' and 'Don Juan.'

**Elegance** ('Glen Dale' x ['Mary Wallace' x 'Miss Lolita Armour'], 1937) is the jewel of the Brownell Sub-zero roses. It is strong-growing and tall, with the most beautiful foliage a rose can boast—dark green, glossy and absolutely immune to disease. The first two names on its family tree both have *Rosa wichuraiana* blood, a wild strain that seems to appear in the background of the best clean-leafed climbers. A few of 'Elegance's' flowers are borne in clusters but the great majority come singly on two- to three-foot stems, ideal for cutting. The color is light clear yellow with a singularly luminous quality, set off to perfection against the dark-toned leave. The form is that of a perfect Hybrid Tea—in fact, when exhibited at the New York Horticultural Society, 'Elegance' was regularly disqualified because the judges thought it was a HT and not a climber.

The plant in the picture was trained on heavy wire mesh fencing four feet high, raised a lawnmower's height above the grass to eliminate the need for hand clipping. It rounded off a corner of the rose garden, forming a light screen between it and the street and giving a measure of privacy without the stern exclusion of a solid fence. The canes stretched 39 feet from one end to the other and yielded 63 dozen cut roses over a period of three weeks, which is more than you'd expect of twenty plants in the course of a year. 'Elegance' has no fragrance, unless you count a cool fresh scent somewhat like that of Romaine lettuce. It has only one flowering period but when you reckon the delight of filling your house and giving away over 750 roses, you may find it easy to forgive its other deficiencies.

**Elegance** is a superlative cut flower, long lasting and beautiful in all stages of development.

# 8
# Planting

## CHOOSING THE SITE

Roses do best in full sun. They will tolerate brief periods of shade—in fact, delicate colors will be kept from bleaching if the hot midday or early afternoon sun is tempered by shadows thrown by tall trees at a distance. However, it is imperative to avoid planting close to trees, hedges or large shrubs whose roots will rob the soil of moisture and nutrients intended for the roses. It should be remembered that our garden roses are man-made plants and as incapable as cage-bred canaries of surviving a struggle for existence in the wild.

In selecting a location for roses, make good air drainage a prime requisite. Freely circulating air promotes quick drying of foliage after wetting by rain or dew. Since water remaining on leaves encourages the germination of fungus spores, the best natural prevention of disease is a brisk flow of air. If your garden is on sloping ground, locate your rose plot near the top of the rise.

Cold air flows downhill like water and draws fresh air after it. Conversely, avoid planting at the foot of a slope, especially in a hollow or frost pocket where cold air settles.

## SOIL PREPARATION

Roses will thrive in many types of soil providing it is reasonably moist but never soggy. The ideal soil is loose, well aerated and fertile. If you are undertaking a large planting, it is advisable to dig the entire plot 18–24 inches deep. As you dig, mix in large quantities of organic material such as peat moss, well-rotted manure or compost, up to one-quarter by volume. Organic material acts as a sponge in sandy soils, absorbing moisture and dissolved nutrients and keeping them from leaching out below the reach of roots. In heavy soils, organic material provides air spaces so that waste gases can readily escape and water and fresh air can move through the soil. In very heavy clay, which is composed of small, tightly compacted particles, the addition of coarse builder's sand will help loosen the soil. Small amounts of bone meal—4 to 5 pounds per 100 square feet—may be worked into the soil but it is advisable not to use chemical fertilizer until roses are well established. The bulky organic matter obviously must be worked deeply into the ground before planting, in amounts sufficient to last the life of the rose, whereas readily soluble chemical fertilizer can be applied on the surface at any time.

If roses are to be planted individually or in small groups, the holes should be dug at least 18 inches wide and 6 inches deeper than the roots when fully extended, usually 18–24 inches. The subsoil, if poor, should be put to another use while the topsoil dug from the hole is mixed with organic matter as just described. With individual holes, be especially careful to break up any hardpan layer at the bottom, otherwise your carefully loosened soil may admit more water than can drain through the impervious hardpan and the rose will drown as surely as if planted in a well.

Digging and enriching the entire plot, or digging individual holes and improving the excavated soil, should be done well in advance of the expected delivery of your roses. There are two benefits of being forehanded: the peat moss and other organic materials can become thoroughly saturated through exposure to weather and the rose roots will suffer less damage from drying if they are planted with a minimum of delay.

## pH FACTOR

The symbol pH (potential of hydrogen) is used to denote the degree of acidity or alkalinity of the soil. A reading of 7 is neutral. Numbers lower than 7 indicate acid soil; above 7, alkaline. Roses do best in soil that is neutral to slightly acid, ideally pH 6.2–6.8. Roses will tolerate a greater degree of acidity than of alkalinity. A soil test will eliminate guesswork. If you send samples to an agricultural college or county agent, specify that you aim to grow roses and ask the testing agency to specify how much lime is needed to counteract overacidity, or the amount of sulphur needed to bring alkaline soil to the optimum degree of acidity.

A pH level is not constant. It should be checked

periodically, especially in cities whose air is heavily pol-
luted by sulphur dioxide derivatives. These contami-
nants may acidify the soil so drastically that a dressing of
lime is needed every two years in order to maintain the
desired pH.

## Mowing Strip

If your rose garden is to have grass paths or if the bed
adjoins a lawn, you will have a continual struggle to
maintain a clean edge unless you install a mowing strip.
Without it, grass invades the rose bed. As it is cut back
with a spade or edging tool, the carefully drawn margin,
whether straight or curved, wavers and loses its neat
line. Also, as you try to mow right to the edge of the
grass, the mower may slip off and bite out a chunk of turf.
A mowing strip preserves the contour of the bed, gives a
firm even surface for the mower wheel to ride on and
reduces maintenance to an occasional clipping of grass
blades that extend over the strip.

The most attractive mowing strips are made with
bricks laid end to end in a trench that leaves the tops of
the bricks slightly below the level of the lawn. In order
to keep grass from pushing between the bricks, install a
fairly deep and quite heavy metal curb between lawn
and bricks. (The lightweight, aluminum curbs sold for
the purpose tend to heave in frost and, being soft, are
difficult to push back into place without bending and
buckling.) Alternatively, heavy plastic can be used to
line the trench. Stretched along the grass side and across
the bottom of the trench, it will be held in place by the
bricks when they are set.

## SPACING

The rule of thumb is to set Hybrid Teas 2 feet apart. If you have done your homework in a rose collection, you will have noted that some roses ('Eclipse,' 'Pascali') are upright and narrow in habit, while robust growers like 'Peace,' 'Proud Land,' 'Hallmark' and 'Fragrant Cloud' send out canes at an angle and therefore require more than average room.

Similarly the spacing of Floribundas is a matter of judgment. Small-scale varieties like 'Yellow Cushion' and 'Angel Face' can be massed only 18 inches apart whereas tall spreading varieties like 'Saratoga,' 'Circus' and 'Apricot Nectar' need considerably more. On the whole, it is better to allow generous elbowroom than to crowd roses, both to insure good air circulation and for your comfort in moving between the plants. When roses are planted too closely, the lower leaves will be shaded and unable to dry quickly after rain or dew, thus becoming prime targets for fungus spores.

The room to allow for climbers depends largely on how you intend to grow them. The method that produces the greatest profusion of bloom is to train them horizontally along a fence with canes stretching in both directions from the base. In this case, you can estimate the space they'll cover by doubling the height given in the catalogue. If they are to be tied to a pillar or trained straight up over an arbor or trellis, they take only planting space plus the extent of their flowering stems.

## TOOLS

While waiting for your roses to arrive, check your tools. In all likelihood you already have standard garden

High-quality secateurs are essential for making clean cuts that promote rapid healing.

tools such as a shovel, rake and trowel. Rose care requires a few special-purpose tools. The most important is a pair of top quality secateurs, that is, pruning shears with two sharp crescent-shaped blades. Cheap pruners with one straight-edged blade and a flat plate are not satisfactory. When the blade gets dull or notched, it munches or crushes a cane, splitting it instead of making a clean cut. Treat your secateurs as you would a razor blade or fine carving knife. Reserve them strictly for fine pruning and don't allow them to be used for rejuvenating overgrown shrubs or cutting up chickens.

For heavier cutting, you will find lopping shears useful—and if you have them on hand, you won't be tempted to use your secateurs for coarse pruning. Lopping shears have two curved blades like those of secateurs but of heavier steel. They are fitted with long handles for added leverage.

If you acquire a property with aged and neglected shrub roses or climbers, you will need a prning saw with a narrow curved blade. This will slide between crowded canes without injuring those you wish to retain. A pruning saw that fits into a slot in the handle is a convenience as you can carry it in your pocket.

Stout leather gloves are an obvious necessity. If you can find gauntlets with long cuffs like an engineer's gloves, you will protect your wrists and forearms as well as your hands. Kneepads—shaped foam rubber cushions with a strap to hold them in place—will shield your knees from contact with stones, stray thorns and wet or cold ground.

## PLANTING

When your roses arrive, open the carton in a shaded place and check the contents against your order list. Cut the strings and remove only the rose you intend to plant first. Keep the others in the box out of sun or drying wind, with roots wrapped in the packing material they came in, usually moist sphagnum moss. If this isn't adequate to cover the roots, wet a burlap bag and use that to wrap them. If roots appear at all dry, plunge them in a tub or barrel of water until ready to plant.

If you haven't prepared the soil in advance, dig the

hole 18 inches wide and deep and mix into the excavated soil and the bottom of the hole approximately one quart of peat moss, one or two handfuls of dried cow manure and a cup of bone meal.

The depth to plant roses depends on the character of your soil. If it is heavy clay or muck and there is no way to improve drainage, the bud union—the knob where scion joins understock—should be just above ground level when the soil settles. Planted deeper, there is likelihood of rotting. In normal well-drained soil, aim at placing the bud just under the surface, covered by no more than an inch of soil.

If possible, enlist a friend or relative to hold the rosebush at the desired depth so that both your hands are free for planting. If you must work alone, you can place a stick or rake handle across the hole and tie the rosebush to it, but the stick will get in the way and the bush is apt to tilt out of plumb when you firm the soil.

Most books about roses tell you to construct a conical mound at the bottom of the hole over which the root system, a perfect cone, is supposed to fit neatly. This method would be admirable if roses were stamped out by machine. In reality, their root patterns are far from uniform: some are one-sided like a fan while others have two long roots angling out like an inverted V. It is necessary to tailor the hole to fit each individual root system, digging deeply and widely enough to accommodate all the roots without bending or cramping. All bruised or broken roots should be cut off cleanly. If your plant has excessively long roots, it is better to shorten the stragglers than to strain your back by digging halfway to China.

When the hole is shaped so that roots can be spread to

*In Loving Memory of*

ANN  H.  RICHARD
December 17, 2002

*God saw you were getting tired*
*And a cure was not to be,*
*So he put his arms around you*
*And whispered, "Come to me."*

*With tearful eyes we watched you,*
*And saw you pass away.*
*Although we loved you dearly,*
*We could not make you stay.*

*A golden heart stopped beating,*
*Hard working hands at rest.*
*God broke our hearts to prove to us,*
*He only takes the best.*

MADE IN ITALY

1639

their full extent, start filling in the prepared soil a little at
a time, working it firmly between and under the roots
with your gloved fingers. When the hole is three-
quarters full, you should check to make sure that no air
pockets remain. To do this, some authorities advise
tramping on the replaced soil. This is a quick method
which may be necessary if you are faced with a large
shipment and limited time to plant it. However, tramping is apt to drive the bud union deeper than you want it.
Also, since you have added organic material to improve
aeration, it seems contradictory to compact the soil.
Tramping is an acceptable shortcut when your soil is
light and sandy but would be inadvisable in heavy clay.
An alternate method is to drill the loose soil with a sharp
stream from the hose, using the force of the water to fill
any voids. This practice, which may remind you nostal-
gically of the way soda fountain clerks stirred an ice
cream soda with a forceful jet from a siphon, is apt to
result in a lot of splattering. If you don't wear glasses,
keep your eyes squinched half shut.

At this time, if the rosebush has settled too deeply, you
can lift it easily through the yielding mud without
damaging the roots.

Continue filling to within a few inches of the surface,
then flood the hole with water. If bubbles appear, air can
be released by gently probing and stirring with a spad-
ing fork. If a second flooding shows no bubbles, let the
water drain away, then fill to grade. In spring planting, it
is advisable to make a saucerlike ring around the hole to
retain water.

Before hilling the roses, examine them carefully and
remove any injured, diseased, crossing or weak
branches. When roses are planted in spring, canes

Steps in planting roses.

should be shortened to 8–10 inches. It may seem barbarous to sacrifice any part of the plump green canes but remember that growth will start before roots have time to become established. If a large number of sprouting shoots demand more water than the roots can supply, you may lose the whole cane instead of just a portion of it.

When you hill your roses, don't dig gullies between the plants but bring earth in from another part of the garden. The earth should be rather lean, that is, as free as possible from fungus-bearing humus particles. In fall, once the canes are partly covered, you can heap any amount of compost or manure—even raw manure—between the hills as this material will not come into direct contact with the canes.

When growth is well started in spring, gradually remove the earth mound. Use the greatest care as the new shoots are extremely brittle and easily knocked off. You may find you can avoid breaking them if you wash away the soil with a gentle stream from the hose.

The canes should now be cut back to an outward-facing bud. This procedure is explained in detail in the notes on pruning (pp. 186–188), but it is so vital to the shaping of a good framework that it can hardly be repeated too often. Canes that grow from an outward-facing bud will of course angle outwards to form the desired open funnel-shaped bush. Conversely, if you cut to inward-facing buds, the stems will grow inwards crossing and tearing each other with their prickles and making a dense, dank, central mass of foliage instead of a well-aerated, sun-inviting bush.

One small final point: it is advisable to remove the metal name tags from bushes and mount them, if

A correctly made cut starting ¼ to ½ inch above an outward-facing bud.

needed, on a nearby stake or wire. The light metal tags swing constantly in the wind, causing the looped wires that secure them to chafe and often kill the cane they hang from.

# 9
# Summer Care

## FERTILIZATION

To speak of "rose food" or of "feeding" roses is to conjure up images of the plants wolfing down gobbets of manure and starving if they don't get it. Neither is true. In the first place, plants have neither mouths nor teeth and can't ingest solid food. They are restricted to a liquid diet of nutrients dissolved in water. Secondly, less than 2% of a plant's "food"—perhaps "building materials" would be a more accurate term—comes from minerals in the soil. The rest, over 98%, is derived from carbon dioxide ($CO_2$) and water ($H_2O$). Plants have the unique ability to transmute these inorganic compounds into starches and sugars and, for good measure, return oxygen to the air. All forms of life on our planet depend on this almost magical faculty of turning stones into bread and providing breathable air. It is a suitably humbling thought that with all our vaunted technological skill, no scientist has been able to duplicate a process that any blade of grass can perform without breathing hard. The

173

bumper sticker that reads, "Have you thanked a tree to-day?" is not far off the mark.

At this point you may ask, "Why fertilize at all?" The reason is that our modern roses are artificial plants, far removed from their tough, once-blooming ancestors which were perfectly capable of holding their own in the wild. Furthermore, we make outrageous demands on our roses. We expect them to keep up a lavish production of outsized blooms for a good six months of the year—and this despite the fact that every time we cut a flower, we take away a portion of the plant's food-manufacturing foliage. In compensation, we must keep a supply of soluble nutrients constantly available so that the plant can quickly replenish what is used—and lost—in the production of flowers.

The subject of fertilization is far from being an exact science. While the need for various elements is established beyond doubt, as is their effect on the development of plant tissues, the subject of the source of these elements is shrouded in tradition, folklore, superstition, hearsay and even deliberate deceit.

One recent misconception holds that nitrogen derived from the decay of organic matter is in some way superior to nitrogen produced in a factory. This is nonsense: nitrogen is an element, a pure chemical substance, unvarying in its properties and identical in function no matter whether it comes from a load of manure or a paper bag. The notion that plants grown with organic fertilizers and without chemical sprays are more healthful or nutritious is, in its crudest terms, a rip-off designed to induce gullible people to pay high prices for wormy apples.

Fertilizers fall into two classes: organic and inorganic or chemical. Since organic fertilizers have historic priority, let's consider them first.

## ORGANIC FERTILIZERS

Before chemical fertilizers were developed, farmers had to replenish their depleted soils by the use of organic materials. One method involved the liberal use of the waste products of living and dead animals—manure, ground bones, blood, offal and fishheads. Since a self-sufficient homestead had at least one plow horse or ox, plus milch cows, pigs and chickens, there was usually a good supply of dung and the by-products of butchering. Another means of increasing the always-volatile nitrogen content of the soil was to plant, grow and then plow under legumes such as peas, vetch, clover or beans. The roots of most legumes are hosts to myriads of symbiotic bacteria, microorganisms with the ability to capture nitrogen from the air and transform it into compounds that can be assimilated by plants and, in turn, by animals. The advantage of green manuring, as the practice is called, is that it puts vegetable matter deep in the soil where it will decay into humus at root level. The disadvantage is that land devoted to a cover crop produces no edible or saleable products for a year.

Since plowing under a cover crop is obviously unsuited to rose gardens, the bulk of organic material must be dug into the soil before planting. This applies especially to peat moss and bone meal, both insoluble and unable to travel in the soil, therefore useless as a top dressing. For the rest, compost and manure (well-rotted barnyard manure if available—if not, the dried product) can be spread generously as a winter mulch between hilled-up roses and then forked into the ground in spring.

The chemical content of organic fertilizers can seldom be determined with any degree of accuracy. In a load of manure, for instance, how can you tell what percentage is animal waste and how much mere straw?

## INORGANIC OR CHEMICAL FERTILIZERS

With chemical fertilizers, there's no guesswork. According to law, the formulation is clearly indicated on the bag. The percentages of the three essential elements—nitrogen, phosphorus and potassium—are given in numbers and always in that order. Thus a 5–10–5 fertilizer contains 5% nitrogen, 10% phosphorus and 5% potassium. A brief examination of the functions of these elements may help you select the formulation that best and most economically serves your purpose. Since you are not growing wheat or sugar beets, you need concern yourself only with the factors that apply to roses.

*Nitrogen.* This is the most vital of all the elements. It is an ingredient of chlorophyll, the green-pigmented cells that capture energy from the sun to carry on the process of photosynthesis. It is chiefly responsible for leaf growth and is therefore used liberally on lawn grasses, lettuce and spinach. Since roses are not grown primarily as foliage plants, a relatively low percentage of nitrogen is recommended. Too much quickly soluble nitrogen can cause serious burning. If applied late in the year, it can stimulate soft growth which, unable to harden before frost, is apt to winter-kill.

*Phosphorus.* This element is particularly effective in promoting flowers, seed and fruit. It also encourages root development. Because of these desirable effects, the fertilizers recommended for roses are high in phosphorus. Since phosphorus, whether supplied in bone meal or superphosphate, is not readily soluble and therefore doesn't move in the soil, it should be dug in deeply enough to be available at root level.

*Potassium.* This element influences root growth and is especially valuable to growers of bulbs and root crops. Its benefit to roses lies in its ability to harden stems, thus counteracting to a degree the tendency of nitrogen to produce soft growth.

The optimum mixture for roses is a matter of contention. Some authorities prefer a nearly equal balance (7–8–5 or 7–7–7). On the other hand, one commercial mixture specifically prepared for roses reads 3–12–6. It is doubtful whether these special formulas—Rose Food, Tomato Food—are worth their extra cost when there are two inexpensive, widely available formulations. One is 10–6–4, with a high nitrogen content especially desirable for use on lawns. The other is 5–10–5, lower in nitrogen and higher in phosphorus and therefore the better choice for roses.

## COST COMPARISON

We have seen that the elements derived from the breakdown of organic material are identical to those from chemical fertilizer. The choice between sources may well be based on a comparison of the cost per pound of each element. For example, it would take 100 pounds of bone meal (analysis 1–11–0) to supply one pound of nitrogen at a cost of about $56.00. Similarly, 100 pounds of dried cow manure (1–0–1) would yield one pound of nitrogen and cost roughly $9.00. The same pound of nitrogen can be supplied by 20 pounds of 5–10–5 at a cost of $5.00.

Bone meal's chief value for rose growers is its relatively high (11%) phosphorus content. It would take just

over 9 pounds of bone meal to yield one pound of phosphorus at a cost of $4.00. Five pounds of superphosphate
(0–20–0) will yield a pound of phosphorus for $1.10.

Considered in terms of cold economics, there is little
justification in buying either bone meal or dried manure.
However, British gardeners—some say they're the best
in the world—are almost mystically dedicated to the use
of bone meal. Certainly it can do no harm.

As for dried manure, it has minimal nutrients and little
bulk but it does have a delicious *growing* sort of smell.
Since fertilization is not an exact science, those who garden for pleasure are free to place emotional and aesthetic considerations ahead of dollars.

### FERTILIZER: WHEN AND HOW MUCH TO APPLY

Newly planted roses should not be given any chemical
fertilizer until midsummer, and then only if they are
growing strongly. It would be injurious to force excessive growth before roots are established sufficiently to
support it.

Established roses should be fertilized three times in a
season: once when the earth mounds are removed, again
in late June after the summer's prodigious production of
flowers, and finally in mid-August to encourage bloom in
September. Species roses and their once-blooming hybrids should be fertilized only at the outset of the season.
Since they have only one flowering period in early
summer, they won't benefit from extra feeding which is
designed to produce repeat bloom. In any case, as wild
or half-wild plants, accustomed to austere growing conditions, they may be spurred to rank vegetative growth if

given too rich a diet. Roses should never be given chemical fertilizer later than August as the resulting succulent growth won't have time to harden before killing frost. After roses are hilled, however, it is beneficial to heap the spaces between the mounds with rough compost and as much manure as you are able to obtain. These slow-acting materials won't spur untimely growth and are dug into the soil in spring when the earth mounds are removed.

The amount of chemical fertilizer to be applied at each of the three summer feedings—2–3 handfuls per plant—may seem small. When you remember that less than 2% of a rosebush's structure comes from the soil, you will realize how little replenishment is needed. To apply dry fertilizer, loosen the soil with a cultivator or trowel and scatter the granules in a band 6–8 inches from the base of the plant. Cultivate again to bury the granules and keep them from washing or spattering on the lower leaves, then water gently and deeply. Be sure to choose a dry day, as any fertilizer that accidentally falls on wet leaves will cause severe burning.

The subject of trace elements is so complex that you should refer to a book specifically dealing with garden soils if you have any doubts. However, it is believed that soils in the Northeast are generally lacking in magnesium, an essential factor in the formation of chlorophyll. If the leaves of your plants are pale or yellowish, try adding a tablespoon of Epsom salts (magnesium sulphate) at the time of spring fertilizing. The for-external-use-only sort costs 34 cents a pound. If leaves turn a richer, deeper green, you've improved your plants and saved the cost of a soil analysis.

## SOIL CONDITIONERS

The bulk organics—peat moss, well-rotted manure and compost—are indispensable for improving the physical structure of the soil. They lighten and aerate heavy soil and improve the water retention of sand; they act as sponges to absorb dissolved nutrients and keep them from leaching out beyond root level; they harbor enormous colonies of beneficial microorganisms; and, as they slowly decay, they yield small amounts of nitrogen and whatever minerals they took from the soil. Think of these bulk organic materials as soil conditioners, not as fertilizers, and you will understand their proper use and function.

The thrifty conservation-minded gardener needn't buy peat moss. Even the smallest garden can have a compost bin, made simply of a circle of chicken wire supported by stakes. Throw into it any disease-free material—leaves, of course, and celery tops, pea pods, cucumber and potato peelings, outside leaves of lettuce, spent flowers—anything that won't smell or attract flies or rodents. If the appearance is displeasing, cover the sides with morning glories or climbing nasturtiums, or train tomato plants to the stakes and let them benefit from the rich ooze from the pile.

This is not a formal compost heap, built up in strictly prescribed layers like a pousse-café. It probably won't heat up enough to destroy weed seeds so be careful not to add them. As to capacity, you'll find that shrinkage of the green material just about keeps up with new additions.

When you think of it, dust a little fertilizer or manure over the pile and soak it thoroughly whenever you water. You needn't bother to turn the pile as complete decomposition is not necessary. If some of the woody material remains in spring, it doesn't matter: you are going to dig in it, and a certain amount of roughage will be beneficial. In addition to making use of vegetable waste, you will find you are putting out less solid waste for the garbage man, a plus mark for any true conservationist.

To sum up the roles of various soil additives, they may be compared in terms of human nutrition. Bulky organic material may be likened to roughage which contains little nourishment but is essential to healthy function. Chemical fertilizers are comparable to supplements such as vitamins or iron, not considered as foods but intended to correct deficiencies in the diet. The vital contribution of water must not be overlooked. Water is not merely a means of keeping a plant from wilting. It is, with carbon dioxide, a plant's chief "food"—building material for plant tissues—and must be supplied regularly, deeply and abundantly.

## WATERING

Water, as we've seen, is a basic building block for plant tissues. Improperly applied to roses, it can promote the growth and spread of fungus diseases. Since the spores of blackspot and mildew require a period of continuous moisture—some authorities say nine hours—in order to germinate, it is obvious that foliage should not be wetted. If this is unavoidable, as may be the case in a mixed planting, plan to water in the morning so that the noonday sun can dry up any persistent drops.

The proper way to water roses, then, is to get water to the roots without wetting the foliage. In a small rose garden, you can use a Waterwand, a pipe with a hose connection at the top and a perforated muffler or expansion chamber at the far end. Without reducing the volume of water, this device tames its force to a soft drizzle. The business end can be held near the base of a bush or between rows without fear of washing soil or splashing foliage. As soil should be wet at least a foot deep, this method takes more time and patience than the average gardener cares to spend standing still.

A similar device, the expansion chamber without a pipe, called a Water Bubbler, is meant to be laid on the ground between rows. It is obviously more difficult to place with precision: in fact, as you swing it between the plants, you may slop water on the leaves. If you are a reasonably competent tinkerer, you can construct a water tamer of your own, using a plastic bottle or jug with the right neck size to accept a hose coupling. Punch or burn holes in the container, fill it with tiny pebbles, clamp on the hose connection and water without splashing.

Another method, and one that takes no attention while operating, is to put a broad plank on the ground—an old breadboard will do admirably—then take the nozzle off the hose and rest its end on the plank. Turn on the water just hard enough to keep a film of water sliding across the plank in all directions and leave it in place until you think the ground is thoroughly saturated. For larger plantings, a soil soaker—a tube of coarse fabric with one closed end and a hose connection on the other—can be threaded between your bushes and left to ooze. This is very satisfactory if one stretch of the soaker will serve all your rosebushes. If it must be moved, dripping mud or coated with clinging particles of mulch, it is a messy nuisance. The flat plastic ribbons meant to throw a mistlike spray on a narrow border or grass walk are much cleaner to handle. Be sure, however, that they are placed upside down, that is, with the holes towards the ground, and not in their position intended for spraying.

## WHEN TO WATER

The anxious novice must learn to resist the temptation to run for the hose whenever the surface of the soil looks dry. "Sprinkling"—frequent and shallow watering—may please the eye but is damaging to plants. If only the top two inches of soil are moist, roots may turn to the surface and scorch when the sun beats down. Conversely, deep-rooted shrubs like roses are deprived of water where it is needed. If a week goes by without a good soaking rain, water your roses and water thoroughly. This rule, like most, has exceptions: newly planted roses and the earth mound that keeps their canes plump should be kept uniformly moist. When strong growth shows that roots have made satisfactory contact with their new environment, the plant is ready to cope with conditions in your garden and needs no more than routine watering.

## THE PROS AND CONS OF MULCHING

There can be no disagreement about the cosmetic value of a mulch such as buckwheat hulls. The uniform texture and rich chocolaty color make a highly flattering background for roses, especially enhancing the clarity of light-toned blooms.

Mulches, according to their proponents, help keep down weeds. This is true in part: while seeds of annual

weeds germinate readily in the soft, moist surface, they
are easily dislodged with a hoe or cultivator before they
sink their roots. However, for perennial weeds, mulches
are worse than useless. The vicious little *Oxalis cornuta,*
the red-leafed sorrel that is thoroughly entrenched in the
BBG rose garden beds and grass paths, finds mulches an
ideal cover. Its invading shoots thrust unobserved under
the surface to start new colonies at a distance.

Mulches conserve water by lessening evaporation
from the soil. In arid regions where watering is restricted, or in extensive plantings where irrigation calls
for more man-hours than can be spared, this one benefit
of mulches will outweigh other drawbacks. There is no
doubt that soil shaded by a mulch remains cooler than
that exposed to full sun. It is believed that cool soil conditions favor root growth and help to keep roses blooming without check even in midsummer.

One of the most serious disadvantages of mulches is
that they make it difficult or impossible to rake up leaves
fallen from rosebushes. Since these leaves are often infected with blackspot or mildew, the moist surface of
the mulch makes an ideal nursery for the germination
and dispersal of spores, thus greatly increasing the
spread of fungus diseases. If a mulch is used, it is advisable to include a thorough spraying of the ground
whenever roses are sprayed with fungicide in order to
destroy the spores on fallen leaves that have lodged in
the mulch.

Each individual gardener must judge the merits of
mulching in the light of his particular garden conditions.
If the decision is to mulch, the best-looking material is
buckwheat hulls. These have the slight disadvantage of
blowing in high winds and of washing on a slope—and if

they pack down in lawn grasses, they are impossible to rake out. In windswept or hilly gardens, pine bark chips may be a better choice. They are coarser in texture but agreeable in color and very long lasting.

Cocoa bean hulls stand lower on the list. Their strong odor conflicts with the fragrance of roses and, if you happen to get the dregs of a shipment, it may be more powder than roughage and will form a hard cake on the surface, cutting off air and water.

Sawdust is readily available and can often be obtained without cost. When fresh, its yellow color is obtrusive, but it soon weathers to a more acceptable neutral tone. Sawdust tends to cake and should be frequently loosened with a cultivator.

Peat moss, though sometimes sold as a mulch, is actually harmful if spread on the surface: it is so highly absorbent that, as moisture is drawn by the sun from the top layer, it may draw water from the soil, leaving it more parched than if exposed.

Woodchips can be used in a pinch but they are coarse and irregular. If the chips contain much leafy material, they may decay so rapidly that they heat the soil instead of cooling it.

Pine needles, often free for the collecting, make an excellent mulch, light, porous and durable, but since they acidify the soil as they decay, frequent liming may be needed.

In the gradual breakdown of mulches, bacteria involved in the process of decomposition will use more nitrogen than they release. Mulches also increase soil acidity in various degrees—pine products, for instance, more strongly than buckwheat hulls. Those who decide to use mulches should plan to increase the amount of fertilizer applied in the three seasonal feedings by a scant handful—half a handful for small plants—and also to check regularly to see if the pH reading has fallen below the recommended 6.2–6.8 level.

## PRUNING

The subject of pruning strikes terror into a novice's heart. Pruning is seen as involving some mysterious formula or species of black magic.

As a fact, nothing could be simpler and more reasonable. The whole purpose of pruning is to shape a rosebush so that it will produce a maximum crop of well-formed flowers and be as nearly as possible immune to disease.

### HYBRID TEA ROSES

Since Hybrid Teas are far and away the most popular type of rose, let's consider their prunning needs first.

When you uncover your roses in spring, look for discolored patches that may indicate brown canker. These are dark brown in color, often sunken and ribbed in texture and may show yellow or tan pustules. Since the canker will ultimately girdle and kill the cane, there is no profit in letting your bush waste vigor in elongating a cane that is going to die. Harden your heart and cut well below the canker, then shut the infected material securely in your garbage can.

The ideal shape for a Hybrid Tea is a funnel or inverted cone with no crowded or crossing branches. The open center of the bush allows sunlight to reach all the foliage and promotes quick drying after rain. The way to achieve this shape is to cut to a bud that points in the

Hybrid Tea before
and after
spring pruning.

direction you want the next shoot to grow. This will usually be outwards. However, young rosebushes are often unbalanced with canes crowded on one side and a void on the other. In this case, choose buds that angle sideways to round out the bush and ensure that each shoot will have ample growing room.

If you are puzzled about locating buds, look in the axil of a leaf (the point at which the leafstalk joins the stem). The shoot that will grow from the bud usually follows the direction of the leafstalk so you can use that for an indicator when leaves are present.

When you have selected a bud that points in the desired direction, place your secateurs ¼–½ inch above it and make a cut that slants somewhat downwards. Take your time and consider the form of the bush as a whole before you cut. Once you've learned the purpose of pruning and the effect you are striving to produce, you will gain confidence in your ability to choose the right place to cut.

The first pruning in spring will generally shorten the canes to 12–18 inches, though you may have to cut farther back if winter damage has been severe. Spring-planted roses should be cut back quite sharply in order to keep top growth in balance with the not-yet-established roots. Once in a while a healthy-looking bush with plump green canes and no sign of disorder will refuse to break dormancy even though its fellows are leafing strongly. First notify your supplier that a replacement may be needed, then uncover the rose and cut it back almost to the base leaving only one or two buds on each stub, then replace the earth mound. This shock treatment will often spur a laggard rosebush into growth. It would be wise to pinch off any flower buds until the plant has fully recovered from the operation.

The beginner may not realize that cutting flowers for the house or removing spent blooms are forms of pruning. The cut should be made with care so that the top bud remaining on the cane points in the direction for best shaping of the plant. Too often, novices fear they may injure their plants if they cut back to strong wood. Instead, they timidly snip off dead flowers just at the neck, the thinnest and weakest part of the cane. This method produces a forest of twiggy growth with many blind (flowerless) shoots and stems too flimsy to support a flower if one should develop.

Newly planted roses should be cut sparingly—in this case, removal of dead flowers is permissible—in order to retain as much foliage as possible to build a strong framework for next year's blooms. With established roses, you must choose between having masses of nondescript flowers or a smaller number of well-formed ones. If you leave many buds on a stem, you will get a quantity of small, often scant-petaled flowers. If you want quality bloom, you must restrict the number of buds. With skyscrapers such as 'Proud Land' and 'Eiffel Tower,' you can often cut yard-long stems. Otherwise, by the end of summer, you'll need a helicopter to observe your roses. For a rule of thumb with tall-growing varieties, count off two leaves from the base of the cane, then select the next outward-facing bud and cut just above it.

Moderate and slow growers should be cut with proportionate restraint. The idea is to keep your rose garden more or less uniform in height, not to have some gawky towering stems and others that seem to be growing in a gully.

Another necessary step in the production of quality Hybrid Tea flowers is disbudding. Some roses are mostly single flowered; others produce more than one bud to a stem. If left to develop, these make an unpleasant congestion instead of one perfect bloom. The unwanted buds are located beside the terminal bud and sometimes also in the axil of the leaves just below it. Remove them simply by tipping them to one side. If this is done early, the stem will heal without a visible scar. Since this is a clean operation, requiring no gloves or tools, it can be an excellent excuse for the gardener to make a leisurely tour of his roses in the cool of the evening.

## SUCKERS

A problem that may afflict all budded or grafted roses, Hybrid Teas included, is suckering, that is, vegetative growth from the understock, usually a wild rose such as *Rosa multiflora*. This occurs infrequently but can be disastrous if not spotted early and promptly dealt with. Suckers can be identified by their leaves which are markedly different from the rose you purchased, usually being lighter in color and having a greater number of small leaflets.

The climbing rose 'Dr. Huey' is sometimes used as understock and can be insidious, as its leaves are indistinguishable from those of other garden roses. If you find your rose is suddenly producing dark red semidouble flowers with white eyes, you'll know that 'Dr. Huey' is taking over—and at this stage of development, it is often too late to oust the intruder and save your bush.

Cutting back a sucker will produce an even denser thicket of unwanted growth which, if neglected, will overwhelm and smother the desirable variety. It is necessary to eradicate the sucker completely where it

**Heirloom,** showing the unsightly congestion that results when Hybrid Teas are not disbudded.

joins the rootstock, leaving no buds to initiate further growth. This can sometimes be done by pulling downwards on the sucker. If it breaks off midway, then you will need to dig alongside the rootstock until you find the sucker's point of origin and cut or pull it off cleanly at the base.

### HYBRID PERPETUALS

Since these are hardier than Hybrid Teas, they are less apt to suffer winter damage. Twiggy growth should be cleared away if this wasn't done in fall. The canes should be shortened as needed to keep the bushes from getting tall and leggy.

## FLORIBUNDAS

With few exceptions, these are grown for mass effect, not for individual blooms. In spring, the canes need to be cut back to firm wood so that the weight of the flower clusters won't cause them to bend or fall over in wet weather. It is advisable to prune all the bushes in a group to a uniform height, with a rounded top to increase the area of visible flowers. When flowers are spent, cut off the whole cluster to induce new flowering shoots and to keep the bush from being choked with brush. As new shoots break from the base, some of the older canes should be removed so that the bush is constantly rejuvenated.

The exceptions noted at the start involve Floribundas whose flowers are so perfect that they resemble miniature Hybrid Teas. 'Fabergé' tops this list, with 'Ivory Fashion' and 'Apricot Nectar' close behind. If you enjoy making small-scale arrangements, you may want to disbud these selected Floribundas to produce individual flowers instead of clusters.

## TREE ROSES

Since these were cut to 8-inch shoots before wrapping, no further pruning is needed in spring unless the tips of some of the shoots have suffered winter damage.

**Apricot Nectar.**

## MINIATURE ROSES

These need little pruning except for removal of dead wood, although it may sometimes be desirable to shorten a shoot if it grows disproportionately tall for the size of the plant.

## CLIMBING ROSES

These are divided into four categories: Ramblers, Large-flowered Climbers (both once- and repeat-blooming), Climbing Hybrid Teas and Pillar Roses.

*Ramblers* are now seldom grown. They bloom only once, their flowers are small and limited in color range and they are excessively prone to mildew. If these are not sufficient deterrents, Ramblers bloom on one-year-old wood. This means that after flowering, all the canes that have bloomed must be cut out and new canes trained up in their place, a needlessly scratchy operation in view of the small reward in flowers.

*Large-flowered Climbers.* These bloom on wood that is two or more years old. Most of them—the old varieties like 'Silver Moon' and 'Dr. W. Van Fleet' especially—are vigorous growers and can rampage over a vast area. When trained flat against a fence, trellis or arbor, the plants take minimal room and justify the space they occupy by their profusion of bloom. Shoots that have flowered should be cut back to two leaves to keep the plant neatly contained against its support.

If not rigorously disciplined, climbers can become soaring brush heaps of dead, fiercely armed wood. Every fall, all dead, aged and unproductive wood should be taken out at the base. For every new cane produced during the year, take out an aging one. This keeps the plant

Climbing roses before and after spring pruning.

from becoming too dense and bulky and also keeps it perennially young.

It will help you train climbers correctly if you recall that they are sprawlers, not true climbers like clematis or wisteria. In the wild, they compete with and overtop other growth by thrusting their canes through shrubs, clinging by their hooked prickles until they break through to the sunlight. The canes then bend over, and it is only this horizontal or drooping portion that produces flowers. Using this tip as a guide, try to train your climbers horizontally. If you let them run straight up the side of a trellis, arbor or porch pillar, the vertical part will show nothing but leaves while the top will be loaded with flowers, too high for enjoyment except by the robins that nest in the elevated thicket.

*Climbing Hybrid Teas.* These make stupendous displays in warm climates but are apt to be killed back severely in cold areas. Since they lose most of their flowering wood, they must spend the summer growing new canes which in turn will be killed before they can bloom. The whole plant can be untied from its support and buried in a trench over winter, but this seems an excessive nuisance when hardy climbers are increasingly available as breeders show renewed interest in this highly desirable section.

*Pillar Roses.* These are climbers of moderate growth, usually not more than 8 feet tall. When tied to a post, they make interesting vertical accents in a rose garden. If the canes are sufficiently long and flexible to be trained in a spiral around the post, so that parts are horizontal or nearly so, you will get more bloom than if the canes rise straight up. Spent flowering stems are cut back to two leaves and the plants are pruned in fall like Large-flowered Climbers.

## SHRUB ROSES

These are mostly the treasured old-fashioned roses: some species, some hybrids, some with pedigrees lost in antiquity. They are so diverse in character that no hard-and-fast rules can be offered. In general, they should not be allowed to grow so tall that their intoxicatingly per-

fumed flowers are ten feet above your head. Old, gnarled woody canes should be removed at the base to make room for new growth, and the tangles of dead twigs that tend to accumulate in the heart of a bush should be cleared away. Dead flowers may be cut off unless you wish to preserve the colorful hips which are highly decorative in winter. Long lax canes may be shortened, although the cascading effect of tumbling blooms is both characteristic and appealing. In dealing with old roses, you must first recognize the natural habit of the plant and then modify it as far as possible to suit your taste.

If you are inventive, you may try new tricks with old roses. Most of them bloom only once, but a few of the newer hybrids—notably the Rugosas—flower throughout the summer. The Rugosa hybrid 'Dr. Eckener' (pictured on page 139) is worth seeking out for its brilliant rose-pink, gold-centered flowers and strong pervasive scent. It makes a somewhat lanky shrub but can be trained with great effect along both rails of a split rail fence. Treated in this way, the horizontal canes will flower at every joint and make an opulent garland to edge your rose garden.

Converting a shrub rose into a climber requires some finesse, as the canes are too rigid to bend once they have hardened. It is necessary to watch for the appearance of new canes and to start tying them as soon as they reach the intended support. Use minimal pressure: when a cane resists, tie it with a loose loop of string in the lowest position it will accept. Next day, test it with a finger. If it has adjusted to the curve and seems willing to dip farther, tighten the string just enough to draw it down another inch or two. If it balks, wait a day and try again. Meanwhile the cane has been lengthening. The outer end, beyond the last tie, will turn upright. If it is allowed to set in that position, it will snap when you try to lay it flat.

Sometimes, despite your care, a cane will snap, often some hours after it has been tied. Don't despair. Assuming that both pieces are immobilized, leave them alone and watch what happens. If the ends are joined by the merest shred of fiber—a trace of tissue no more substantial than the skin that remains when you break a stalk of asparagus—the break may heal itself. The raw cuts first callus over, then the callus thickens and spreads over the gap until it cements the ends solidly together. The power of regeneration is so nearly miraculous that you may be tempted to snap a cane on purpose in order to refresh your sense of wonder.

# 10
# Pests and Diseases

Nobody likes to spray. It's a job that invites procrastination. The very reminder on your schedule of garden chores is likely to trigger a tremendous burst of weeding or other diversionary tactic. As a fact, the time spent in avoiding the job may be greater than the time it takes to perform it.

In a small rose garden where plants are widely spaced and air circulation is free, you may escape the common fungus diseases, blackspot and mildew, at least for a while. However, the onset of a spell of high humidity with intermittent rain or fog will leave rose foliage and buds gray and distorted with mildew or the leaves disfigured by blackspot. These diseases can't be cured once the fungus has invaded plant tissues. The only method of ensuring clean foliage is prevention, which means keeping the leaves coated with a fungicide such as Phaltan. Though good culture will reduce, if not entirely eliminate, fungus infection, it is no guard against pests such as aphids and Japanese beetles. Against these, you have a choice of adding an insecticide (Malathion, Isotox, Sevin) to your routine antifungus spray, or spraying for insects only when the pests appear. If you are conservation-minded, you may prefer the latter method as there is less danger of killing beneficial insects such as ladybugs, lacewings or bees if the insecticide is used only when actually needed.

Before you buy any equipment, you should weigh the comparative conveniences and hazards of spray versus dust. Using dust is perhaps easier than spraying as it involves no dissolving or stirring. However, dust borne on a relatively weak stream of air is less able to penetrate dense foliage than a forcefully propelled liquid, and consequently may fail to coat every leaf. Again, dust may not adhere to dry foliage. On the other hand, it is not likely to burn leaves as liquid sprays may do if carelessly measured or applied in hot sunny weather. As to the safety factor, clouds of dust are more apt to be windborne than the heavier drops of spray and, when inhaled, may cause irritation in those with sensitive respiratory systems. Conversely, liquids are more readily absorbed by the skin, though this can be obviated in part by wearing rubber gloves.

Aerosol sprays are not recommended, primarily because of their damaging effect on the atmosphere. Since they will spray only in an upright position, it is difficult to coat the underside of lower leaves. If the distance is misjudged, the propellant can cause severe damage to leaves by burning.

A few general rules apply to both methods. Follow the manufacturer's directions. Don't imagine that if one teaspoon per gallon is recommended, a tablespoon will do a better job. Don't spray in hot sun or when the temperature is over 80°F. Keep all chemicals securely locked out of reach of children. Wash thoroughly with soap and a brush after using, or immediately if any of the concentrate or solution gets on your skin.

There are many preparations under different trade names. Since it is difficult for the novice to evaluate them by reading labels and advertising claims, it may be helpful to outline the program tested and used at the BBG.

## DORMANT SPRAY

A dormant spray of lime-sulphur is applied early in the year to control stem canker as well as to destroy scale and any insect eggs that may have overwintered on the canes. Spraying can be timed for early March on a day when the temperature is above freezing. It must never be used after mid-April when leaf buds start to open: the material is extremely caustic and will shrivel any new growth. Lime-sulphur should not be used where it will hit or drift onto painted wood such as house walls, trim or trellises. Since it is usually sold in five-gallon cans, it is obviously intended for professional use in large rose plantings. The home gardener is advised to use a dormant oil spray which is less caustic (but inevitably less effective) and is not damaging to painted surfaces.

## DISEASES

*Powdery mildew.* This parasite affects roses as well as other commonly grown ornamentals such as lilacs and phlox. Since its spores are always in the air, no amount of sanitation will prevent its spread. The spores need only

Powdery mildew.

moist air, not an actual drop of water, in order to germinate, so your best efforts in careful watering and in providing good air circulation may be negated by a spell of
high humidity.

The first symptom of mildew attack is a blistering of
the leaf surface, especially on tender new growth. Next,
the affected part becomes covered with a fine network of
white threads (mycelia) which sink sucking devices
(haustoria) into plant cells. From this feltlike surface,
chains of gray-white spores grow at right angles, thus
producing the characteristic powdery effect. Since the
spores are carried by wind currents, infection spreads
rapidly until foliage, buds and bud stalks are blanketed
and distorted by the parasite.

At the BBG, roses are sprayed every week to ten days
from the start of the growing season. The spray is composed of Isotox mixed alternately with one of two fun-

gicides: Benlate one time, Phaltan the next. In dry weather, spraying may be reduced to once every two or three weeks, with a precautionary spraying in advance of any predicted rain or onset of high humidity. Hot dry weather, however, encourages the proliferation of spider mites whose control is outlined later in the chapter.

Isotox is a wide-spectrum mixture combining Sevin (a contact insecticide), Kelthane (an acaricide for spider mite control), and Metasytox R (a systemic insecticide and acaricide). Because of its systemic ingredient, Isotox should not be used in a home garden where vegetables, herbs or fruits are grown. In this situation, substitute Sevin or Malathion or, for complete assurance, the vegetable derivative pyrethrum-rotenone which can be used on food crops up to the day before harvest.

*Blackspot* may not be as universally present as powdery mildew but its effect on roses is even more devastating. The first sign is a sooty spot often surrounded by a yellow halo. As the infection advances, the leaf turns yellow and falls. Severely infected plants may be defoliated by midsummer and, as a result, so seriously weakened that they become targets for winter injuries such as dieback and stem cankers.

Blackspot spores are transmitted by drops of water (rain or a carelessly used hose) bouncing from the ground or from an infected to a clean leaf. In the case of blackspot, sanitation is an important control measure. In a small garden, infected leaflets can be picked into a bag and destroyed—but in doing so, be careful not to brush healthy foliage with the disease-bearing leaves and be sure to wash your hands thoroughly before touching rose plants again. It is also important to rake up any infected leaves that may fall to the ground.

Blackspot.

Here again the question of mulching has its pros and cons. A mulch will undoubtedly help to deaden the force of water and keep raindrops from splashing. On the other hand, it is difficult to remove all infective material when leaves fall and sift into the mulch. If a mulch is used, it would be wise to give it a good drenching when you use a fungicidal spray on the plants themselves. This should be done every week in the early season, with a spacing out of every eight or nine days in midsummer. Phaltan is outstandingly effective in preventing blackspot.

*Cankers* occur in plants that have been weakened by

blackspot, physical injury or poor nutrition. Brown canker, the most common variety, starts as small, reddish spots on the cane, then increases to sunken, barklike patches that ultimately encircle the stem and kill it. All visible cankers should be removed below the infection during spring pruning. The infected material should be destroyed and the pruning tool disinfected with alcohol or clorox after use. The routine fungicidal spray should control further infection. Some authorities believe that moisture-retaining winter covering—straw, hay, leaves, even earth—may increase the incidence of cankers. For a discussion of the question of whether or not to hill roses for winter protection, see pages 212–215.

## PESTS

Many animals, ranging in size from spider mites and aphids to rabbits and deer, are partial to roses. Relatively few suburban gardeners are afflicted with deer (for control, consult your county agent), but rabbits are common especially where dogs are not permitted to run at large. Rabbits are not ordinarily serious menaces to roses, but when their normal browse is covered by snow, they may gnaw bark or chew canes. One particularly voracious rabbit stripped all the bark off 'Dr. Eckener' whose lower canes, trained along the bottom rail of a fence, were within easy reach. Considering the fierce armament of Rugosa roses, it is difficult to understand how a rabbit could have taken a second bite when the first must have filled its mouth with prickles. Nevertheless it persisted until every shred of bark was gone from snowline to the top rail. It was fortunate that snow was deep enough to protect the base of the plant, from which new shoots grew in spring, but the entire top was lost. It took several years to restore the plant to its original fullness. Hilling roses, where snow is not a dependable cover, would serve the same purpose of protecting the vital base of a rosebush. For the upper part of the canes, you can construct a cage of chicken wire or thrust Christmas tree branches, needle side out, into the ground at an angle and tie their tips together above the plant. Your local garbage man will be most happy to drop off discarded Christmas trees. In fact, you had better specify the number you want or your lawn may be piled to the second-story windows. Climbing roses can also be swathed in evergreen branches, tied securely so the wind won't dislodge them. To figure how high the protection should extend, start with the depth of the heaviest snow you are likely to get and add the height of a rabbit on tiptoe.

*Aphids* are a very prevalent pest of roses as well as of innumerable ornamental plants. On roses, these soft-bodied insects are usually pale green and almost translucent and may escape notice until they have built up a substantial colony. Those that suck the juice from bud stalks can easily be rubbed out between thumb and finger. Others that congregate between the tightly folded leaves of developing shoots must be hit by a penetrating insect spray.

Since newborn aphids become mothers in a matter of a few days, the rate of increase can be astronomical. Try to hit them when they first appear so you won't have to deal with a succession of broods. It may be necessary to spray every day until the colony is wiped out. Malathion, Isotox, Sevin, and the least toxic insecticide, pyrethrum-rotenone, are all effective.

*Japanese beetles* have been on the decline in recent

years but there is disturbing evidence that a new population may be building up. These handsome, bronze-green beetles are voracious feeders, ganging up in great numbers on roses—especially light-colored ones—and chewing the flower to rags. Spraying is only a partial protection. Spray coats the outside of a closed bud, but as the flower starts to open, beetles swarm into the interior and eat its heart out without getting a dose of poison.

If beetles are few and you are not squeamish, you can crack their shells by pinching both sides towards the middle. However, if beetles are present in swarms, obviously you can kill only one while the others fly away. In this case, fill a coffee can partway with water, float some oil or kerosene on top and keep the can and its lid handy in the rose garden. In morning and late afternoon, when beetles are sluggish, go round the garden, hold the can close under an infested rose and tap it from above with the lid. Beetles usually drop when disturbed and will land in the oily trap. If they fly upwards, the lid will deflect them so they bounce back into the can. A few will escape by flying sideways but the majority will churn slowly in the greasy bath until they drown. It is astonishing what satisfaction even the gentlest-hearted gardener will derive from the sight.

Systemic poisons, which are absorbed into plant tissues through roots or leaves, should in theory be an effective way of enabling roses to bite back when bitten. Unfortunately, systemics are ineffective in controlling either chewing or sucking insects on roses, as repeated tests at the BBG rose garden have demonstrated. In the home garden, where food crops and herbs are often grown, the use of systemics is not recommended. There is a chance that plants containing systemics could be thrown on the compost heap, while contaminated soil may be transferred to other areas of the garden during planting or cultivating. In addition to the sprayer reserved for safe insecticides such as pyrethrum-rotenone, another must be set aside for systemic poisons. Since human error has not been outlawed, there is a possibility of serious results if the sprayers are switched.

Japanese beetles.

FRANK J. BOWMAN

*Earwigs* are becoming a significant pest in the Northeast. These are slender brown insects with curved forceplike appendages at the tail end of the abdomen. They are largely nocturnal in habit, burrowing into a bud and feeding out of sight until the petals fall in shreds. Earwigs are too swift moving to be caught. When disturbed, they drop to the ground and scurry under any loose cover. To control them, drench the soil of the rose bed with Diazinon.

*Rose midges* in the adult form are minute, yellow-brown flies that lay their eggs on rosebuds or on the stalk just beneath. The larvae, as they feed, totally destroy young buds and cause more mature ones to grow crooknecked. The first indication of an invasion of midges is the discovery of buds pointed at right angles to their stem. When you notice such deformed buds, look for tiny scars on the inner surface of the curve. These scars will confirm the presence of midges.

A second symptom is so inconspicuous that you will not be likely to notice it unless crooked necks have already spread the alarm. If you examine your rosebushes closely, you will find small black dots on the tips of young shoots just below the point where the flower bud would be expected to appear. The bud will not develop: cut it off, together with all crooknecks, above the first outward-pointing leaf. Use a plastic bag to contain the infested material so that no maggot can wriggle free and find sanctuary in the soil.

Maggots drop to the ground to pupate, then emerge as adults to repeat the cycle, which takes as little as two to three weeks. While they are feeding within the bud, maggots are secure from contact by spray. However, they can be killed in the soil by a drenching spray of Diazinon which has the added benefit of checking earwigs and the destructive root weevils that work unseen below ground. With a determined two-pronged attack—a search-and-destroy campaign against maggots in the bud and a drench of poison to kill them in the ground—you should be able to eliminate the midges and enjoy normal roses in the next wave of bloom.

*Scale insects* and spider mites are two of the most insidious enemies of roses because they are difficult for the uninitiated to recognize. Scale insects look like tiny pebbles or—more commonly on house plants than on roses—like tufts of cotton. The female scale insect constructs a shell under which she can suck plant juices without fear of predators and from which her prolific broods of young creep to start life on their own. At this stage they are susceptible to insecticides but the precise timing is difficult to hit on. The best control is a dormant spray of lime-sulphur (1 part liquid concentrate to 9 parts of water). For small gardens, use a dormant oil spray. Both must be applied before the buds start to break.

Infestations of scale are often found on Japanese cherries, old lilac canes or neglected, overgrown climbing and shrub roses. These reservoirs of infestation should be cut to the ground, as should heavily encrusted canes of garden roses.

*Spider mites* are not true insects though they act like them. The first sign of their presence is a stippling of light-colored dots on the surface of rose foliage. The leaf takes on a rusty reddish tinge before browning and falling. If you turn an infected leaf over, you will see a network of fine webs. Unless they are moving actively, you may need a hand lens to pick out the mites themselves: they are minute specks of reddish-tan or cream color. It is ironic that in hot dry weather, when the gardener can relax vigilance against fungus diseases, spider mites stage a population explosion. To control them, spray at weekly intervals with the miticide Kelthane, which should be used separately, not mixed with other spray materials. Use special care to hit the underside of every leaf as this is where spider mites congregate.

The important factor in the management of diseases is to forestall them by keeping rose foliage constantly coated with fungicide. In the case of insects, early detection and immediate spraying, continued until the pests are eliminated, will free you from fighting recurrent broods all summer.

If you encounter some uncommon and unrecognized insect problem, consult the definitive book on the subject, *Anyone Can Grow Roses* by Cynthia Westcott. Both the fourth edition (Van Nostrand, 1965) and the paperback (Macmillan, 1967) are out of print but can be found at a library. Both printings contain references to DDT and Chlordane, substances now banned, but it is easy to translate these into their approved equivalents, Sevin, Malathion or pyrethrum-rotenone. If you want a more up-to-date but less rose-oriented book, turn to Dr. Westcott's encyclopedic *The Gardener's Bug Book* (Doubleday, 1973) which has the advantage of colored illustrations to help clinch the identity of your particular pest.

# 11
# Winter Care

The question of whether or not to hill roses is one that can only be decided on the basis of your particular climate and soil type.

1. Snow is the ideal insulation against drying wind and severe cold. In areas where snow comes early and lies long and deep, your roses need no other covering.

2. If snowfall is scanty and the ground stays solidly frozen all winter, it is advisable to hill your roses. This is done both to protect against extreme cold and to keep cutting winds from drying the canes at a time when roots are locked in ice and unable to take up water to restore what is lost.

3. If you have freeze-and-thaw winters with quickly melting snow and much rain, don't hill. Hilling can be especially harmful if your soil is heavy moisture-retaining clay. Wet earth in prolonged contact with rose canes will encourage fungus diseases, in particular the damaging stem cankers.

Snow is the ideal winter protection.

## BUSH ROSES

In the New York City area, winter temperatures seldom go below 5°F. Periods of snow alternate with sodden thaws and heavy rain. Roses are not hilled at the BBG. Winter losses are minimal, consist mostly of varieties unsuited to the climate, such as 'Oregold,' or plants with weak constitutions such as 'Sterling Silver' or 'John F. Kennedy.'

If you have mulched your rose beds and intend to hill the bushes, you are faced with another decision: should you bury the mulch and let it break down into humus or rake it up and store it for use the following season? If you have mulched with sawdust, which you presumably got free of charge, the decision to bury it is easy. In any case, it will probably have broken down to an extent that makes it unusable. Buckwheat hulls can perhaps be salvaged, at least the top layer which may still be intact. Pine bark chips which break down very slowly can be raked up and stored for reuse. If you decide to leave the mulch in place, rake it away from the base of the bush so that no soggy material remains in contact with the canes.

Delay hilling roses until you have had several hard frosts but do it before there is likelihood of having the ground freeze solid. Exposure to early frosts, with temperatures in the 20s, will help to harden the canes. Earth mounds built while the weather is still mild may offer tempting shelter for mice, whereas if you wait until cold weather has settled in, vermin will have found winter quarters elsewhere.

Whether you hill or not, you should examine your rose-bushes as soon as frost has stripped them of leaves. Now you can get a clear look at the structure of your plants and do some corrective pruning. Take off weak shoots, brushy twigs, crossing branches and any that show signs of disease. Long canes should be shortened by half to keep them from whipping in the wind, since their movement may open spaces through which freezing air can penetrate to the roots. With lower-growing roses, take off one-third. This is blind pruning, that is, cutting without regard to the position or direction of buds. Fine pruning in fall would be a waste of effort as the tips of canes are likely to be winter-killed and would need to be recut in spring when painstaking selective pruning takes place.

When you hill roses, don't be tempted to scoop up earth from between the bushes. This would defeat the

purpose of hilling by exposing bud union and roots to cold and also to possible rotting from standing in puddles of water. Instead, bring in earth from another part of the garden where the soil is lean and as free as possible from humus particles. The holes you dig can be filled with garden refuse—spent annuals, leaves, worn-out string beans—well dusted with lime and weighed down by a few inches of soil. When you uncover your roses in spring, use the soil to fill the excavations and have ready-made planting sites for greedy-rooted, moisture-loving plants such as tomatoes and cucumbers.

As you shovel earth onto your roses, pat the growing mound firmly to exclude air pockets and keep the canes from swaying in strong winds. In moderate climates, a 6–8 inch mound will probably be sufficient. In areas where temperatures fall to zero or below, you should increase the height of the mound, as any protruding portion of cane will almost certainly be killed. Roses will recover if the bud union and a few buds on each cane are preserved. A greater length may conserve some nutrients stored in the cane and also give you greater choice of buds when it comes to spring pruning.

In extremely cold climates, loss of water from projecting canes can be lessened by heaping the mounds with salt hay; by making a tepee of Christmas tree branches thrust cut-end into the earth and tied together at the tips; or by both together. The evergreen branches serve to discourage rabbits and also add some welcome color to the lifeless winter rose garden.

When hills are completed, you should fill the valleys between the mounds with compost or manure or both. This is to be lightly forked into the soil in spring when roses are uncovered.

## CLIMBING ROSES

Ramblers and most large-flowering climbers are hardy at least to zero and need no protection in moderate climates, though you may want to mound earth over the base as insurance against an exceptionally cold winter. In a particularly exposed site, the canes may be covered with bundles of cornstalks or salt hay tied securely, or sheltered by a windbreak of burlap. If this is not adequate for your climate—and rose growers in the vicinity are your best source of information—then you will have to cut the canes from their support and peg them along the ground. The base must be heavily mounded while the canes are covered with soil or salt hay.

As noted on p. 10, climbing sports of Hybrid Teas are no hardier than their parents. Since they bloom on wood that is a year or more old, their canes must be protected from freezing if they are to flower the following season. The best protection is to remove the canes from their support, peg them to the ground and cover the entire plant with soil.

## STANDARD OR TREE ROSES

These are Hybrid Teas or Floribundas budded on a tall stem. The sensitive bud union is held high in the air, exposed to cutting winds and freezing temperatures. Since the head can't be hilled in its lofty position, one method is to bring it to ground level. This operation, called trenching, is a rather drastic one. First, the earth is loosened on one side of the roots. A foot-deep trench is dug on the opposite side and the whole plant gently eased down into it and buried.

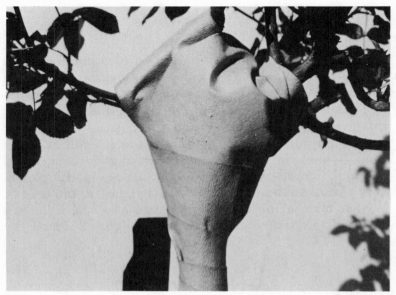

The bud union is wrapped in burlap strips as the first step in preparing a tree rose for winter.

## CRANFORD ROSE GARDEN METHOD

Here at the BBG we have developed a method of protecting tree roses without bending the trunk, disturbing the roots or disrupting a landscaped area by digging a trench.

Around Thanksgiving time, cut back the canes to 8–10 inches. Provide yourself with scissors, soft cotton string and rolls of tree wrap, either specially treated paper or the 4-inch-wide burlap used at the BBG. One roll is sufficient for two or more tree roses.

The first step is to wrap the trunk together with its stake. Beginning at ground level, give the free end of the wrapping material a few turns around the bases of trunk and stake and continue winding in a gradual upward spiral, making sure that each turn overlaps the one below it. When you reach the crown, pass the roll between the canes and over the top of the bud union. Pull the strip down, loop it around the base of the nearest cane, then pull it up and across the top in another direction. Repeat the process until the knob is completely covered. Tie the wrapping snugly just below the crown, at the base and halfway between, then cut off the excess.

Next take an ordinary burlap bag and roll its edges back in the shape of a holeless doughnut. Place the

The root area is mulched with leaves.

DAPHNE DRURY

closed bottom of the bag on top of the rose and roll the edges down, easing them over the ends of the canes, until the bag is fully opened. Twist the loose edges of the bag around the trunk and tie it securely.

The final step is to protect the roots. Take 5 feet of corrugated aluminum edging, 5–8 inches wide, and bend it in a circle with the base of the rosebush in its center. Clamp or overlap the ends and secure the ring with stakes driven into the ground to keep it upright. Fill the ring with dry leaves—oak leaves are ideal as they retain their crispness, but avoid soft leaves such as maple which pack down into a soggy layer. When Christmas trees are discarded, clippings from their branches make an airy extra covering and are pleasing to the eye.

# 12

# Growing Roses in Containers

Growing roses in containers is difficult because it is wholly unnatural. The roots of a potted plant are cut off from direct contact with the earth and its reservoir of water. The risk of drying out is increased when plants are grown on a rooftop or unprotected balcony, exposed to high winds that whip moisture from leaves and soil. In winter, plants in containers are subjected to freezing not merely from the top surface but from the sides and bottom as well.

## WINTER PROTECTION

Winter protection is both the most crucial and the most exacting factor in keeping container-grown roses from year to year. Gardeners should know in advance what this specialized form of rose growing entails before they tackle its cultural demands. Some gardenless gardeners would rather have roses in containers than none at all, while others find that the chores of maintenance are far outweighed by the pleasure of having roses within reach of one's lounge chair.

The problem of winter protection is simplified if you have a cold frame, a garden where potted roses can be sunk in the ground, or an unheated garage or glassed porch for storage. Difficulties multiply when you take up the challenge of growing roses on a rooftop or exposed balcony where protective measures must be improvised without recourse to insulating soil or enclosed storage space.

To start with the easier situation, clay pots, which would break if exposed to freezing in the open, can be wintered safely in a cold frame. Lacking a frame, you can sink the pots an inch or two above the rim in a vacant spot in the garden and hill earth over the base of the rosebush. The finish of wooden tubs would be marred by prolonged contact with earth. The rosebush can be tipped out of the tub, temporarily planted with the bud union an inch or so below the surface, and then hilled. If you want to retain the dimensions of the earth ball for easy replacement in its tub in spring, wrap the soil with a layer of salt hay.

The successful wintering of roses on a roof or balcony is a test of ingenuity. Since they are divorced from contact with moist earth, give them a thorough watering before the soil freezes and another during the January thaw if the soil looks at ll dry. Choose the most protected spot available, in a corner or against a wall that will help break the force of the wind. Bunch the containers as closely as possible, chinking the spaces between them with whatever cold-repelling material you can obtain or improvise.

The materials commonly recommended for winter

protection include salt hay, peat moss, sawdust, ground cork, excelsior or the fiberglass batts used to insulate attics. All of these have the disadvantage of absorbing and retaining water. When water, an effective heat conductor, replaces the vital air spaces, the insulating property of the material is reduced or destroyed. If you have ever lifted a hot skillet with a damp potholder, you know by painful experience how quickly water transmits heat.

In choosing a method of protecting your plants, try to duplicate the construction of a down jacket or sleeping bag: a waterproof casing puffed out with loose fibrous material which creates multiple cells of nonconducting dead air. Of the materials listed, excelsior has the best air-trapping ability with the least bulk, plus enough stiffness to keep it from packing down. If you can find a source of excelsior, fluff it up and stuff it into plastic garbage bags. Fold over the open edges of the bags several times and staple the folds to exclude water. These relatively small bags are useful to pack between containers as you fit them into a group. If the sides taper towards the base, as those of most wooden tubs do, take especial care to fill the gaps between them.

If you can't find excelsior, you can fall back on crumpled newspaper which is just as effective in trapping air but lacks the resilience of shredded wood. One of the advantages of using available no-cost material is that you needn't bother to find storage space in spring but can discard the whole assemblage without a qualm.

The final outer blanket that surrounds the cluster of containers can be made by stuffing larger bags and sealing the ends. These can be heavy plastic rubbish bags for durability or the better-shaped dry cleaners' bags, though these are somewhat flimsy and may not hold up on a windswept roof. Anchor the outer covering to the ground with bricks or planks so no cold draft can sneak under it, then secure the whole bundle with a network of cords, a chicken wire fence or a wrapping of burlap.

The surface of the soil should be well mulched with peat moss or sawdust. Prune the tops of the canes as directed on page 214, then tie them together and wrap them in burlap or roof them with a tepee of Christmas tree branches. For tree roses, in case anyone is brash enough to attempt growing them on a roof, follow the instructions on pages 216–219.

## TYPES OF CONTAINERS

If this recital of difficulties hasn't dampened your enthusiasm for growing roses in containers, we can go on to a discussion of the best types and sizes. As mentioned earlier, clay pots—while ideal for porosity—are apt to crack unless buried or wintered in a cold frame. Potted miniature roses are an exception: they can be grown as windowsill plants if given a sunny exposure not immediately over a radiator, with pots set on pebbles in a water-filled tray. Miniatures can thrive in smaller pots in proportion to the size of the variety, but a 12 by 12 inch clay pot is the minimum for a standard-sized rose.

It is important to remember that roots need air as well as water. For this reason, and also because they are apt to have inadequate drainage holes, metal or cement containers are not recommended. Round wooden tubs, 12 by 12 inches, and octagonal tubs 13 inches high and 15 inches across are satisfactory for roses of standard size. For climbers, the tub should be no smaller than 18 inches high and 33 inches in diameter. Heavy containers can be set on wheeled dollies before they are filled with soil. They can then be turned readily to present their best face to the viewer and also to keep the plant from growing one-sided if it stretches to reach the sun.

For window boxes or troughs intended to top or line the base of a wall, allow a width of 13 inches, a depth of 14 inches and whatever length the site calls for. If the space to be filled is long, it is better to construct a series of boxes rather than a single elongated one which might break in handling, if indeed you can move it at all.

## SOIL

To insure good drainage, start with enough soil to fill three-quarters of the container. Make up the remaining one-quarter by mixing in equal parts of coarse sand and either peat moss or compost, plus two handfuls of bone meal or dehydrated cow manure. If you must use packaged soil, which when wet has the consistency of chocolate pudding, increase the amount of sand to half the volume.

## PLANTING

For best results, ask to have your roses shipped for arrival two or three weeks after frost has left the ground. In the New York area, this means the end of March or the beginning of April. Spring planting will enable the roots to become well established before they must undergo the rigors of winter in a container.

On the bottom of each container, place two or three inches of drainage material. This may be potsherds, gravel or pebbles, with the addition of charred wood from your fireplace. (Avoid briquettes which are often impregnated with chemicals.) It is good practice to spread a layer of sphagnum moss over the drainage material. This serves to keep the soil mixture from sifting down and clogging the air spaces and also provides a reservoir of deep moisture. If you can't get sphagnum moss, try nylon stockings, slit and opened flat. These will act as filter but not of course as a store of water.

The rosebush should be planted according to directions on page 167, with one exception. Since the hole can't be deepened to accommodate overlong roots as is possible in the open ground, cut straggling roots so they will fit the container without bending.

Fill the container to within two inches of the rim to facilitate thorough watering. When planting is finished, the bud union should be covered with an inch of soil in cold climates and level with the surface where winters are mild. After planting, soak the soil mixture until water runs out of the drainage holes in the bottom of the container. If bubbles indicate air pockets, probe gently with a stick or kitchen fork to release them.

## SUMMER CARE

Container-grown roses should be kept in the sunniest spot available, with an absolute minimum of four hours direct sun if the plants are to bloom. If the terrace faces south or southwest, some broken shade at midday will keep delicate-colored roses from fading. Shade can be supplied by a thin-foliaged tree such as a honey locust, by a climbing rose on a frame or by a trellis of morning glory or similar vine.

In adjusting soil moisture, it is necessary to strike a balance between parching and drowning. An inch of organic mulch—peat moss, compost, coffee grounds, tea leaves, dried manure—worked into the surface will help reduce water loss on days of hot sun and drying wind. Pebbles or marble chips can be used to insulate the surface. Buckwheat hulls are attractive but apt to blow in windswept places. Perhaps the best covering is the pine bark mulch available at large garden centers. Your local florist, who makes trips to the wholesale market at least twice a week, will usually oblige by filling—and perhaps even delivering—special orders for materials not regularly carried in his shop.

Of the two extremes—powder dry and soaking wet—the latter may be the more damaging. Certainly it is harder to control. If torrential three-day rains are forecast with only moderate winds, you can improvise shelter for your roses: stack them under a porch table and drape it with a plastic tablecloth, painter's dropcloth or shower curtains. If you haven't a suitable table, you can rig a pup tent by lashing a mop handle to the backs of two chairs and draping a waterproof sheet over it. Be careful to stretch out and weigh down the free edges so no pocket of water can form as this would press on the roses and break their canes.

If a hurricane or gale winds are predicted, it is better to lay the containers gently on their sides than to let them blow over by force. To keep soil from spilling, crimp heavy aluminum foil around the base of the bush and over the rim of the container, tying it in both places for added security. To keep the canes from whipping, you can group the laid-over containers and cover them with a plastic sheet, being careful to tuck the loose edges under the heaviest containers so no wind gusts can rip them loose.

For ultimate protection, if you have a wide doorway, a shallow doorsill and a strong back, borrow a hand truck from the janitor and cart the roses indoors until the storm blows itself out.


## FERTILIZING

Fertilizing container-grown roses follows the same schedule as that used in the open garden. A 7–8–5 formulation is recommended by professional rosarians. As this is seldom available in retail stores, the commonly stocked 5–10–5 will give quite satisfactory results. The amount of fertilizer to use depends to a great extent on how quickly and thoroughly containers and soil will drain. If soil is sandy and easily flushed, you can use up to a handful of fertilizer at a time. If drainage is sluggish, a build-up of salts may occur which is injurious to roots. In this case, be sparing with chemical formulations and make up the deficit with organic fertilizers: fish, seaweed or manure tea (dried manure steeped in water), which grizzled gardeners vow will intensify the color of roses whether grown in containers or in the open ground. When chemical fertilizers are used, scatter them evenly, scratch into the top inch of soil and water well to distribute the dissolved nutrients through the soil mass.


## REPOTTING

When a rose has outgrown its container, it should be repotted in late autumn. Prune the bush, tip it out of its pot, and scratch away as much old soil as possible without injuring the roots. Old woody roots can be cut off to stimulate growth of vital new roots. Replant the rosebush in fresh soil with the usual admixture of sand and organic material. Some authorities recommend re-

newing the soil in this manner every three years
whether or not the plant needs a larger container.

## SPRAYING

If your terrace is at ground level and you grow other
roses in the garden, you will need to observe the same
spray schedule for container-grown roses as for those in
the open beds. A mixture of Isotox and either Benlate or
Phaltan will control insects and fungus diseases. However, if you grow herbs or vegetables, it would be safer to
use a pyrethrum-rotenone insecticide instead of the systemic Isotox in order to avoid possible contamination of
food crops.

Roses grown on a windy rooftop are not apt to be trou-
bled by flying insects. Rapid drying of foliage decreases
the incidence of fungus diseases. If the rooftop gardener
chooses roses according to the standards that follow, he
may well be spared the necessity of spraying.

## SELECTION

Roses for container growing must be able to pass close
and constant inspection throughout the entire outdoor-
sitting season. Varieties that stop blooming in the heat of
summer, or exhibit unsightly symptoms of blackspot or
mildew, or grow leggy and bare at the bottom, may be
tolerated in massed rose beds. When closely grouped,
their deficiencies may be concealed by their fellows. In
a freestanding container, all flaws are on public display.

If you choose your roses by their catalogue portraits
only, you may be sadly misled. Take 'Angel Face,' for
example. Its rich old-rose perfume and neatly imbricated
lavender petals edged with shocking pink would seem to

commend it as a charming end table companion. However, its foliage is so critically susceptible to fungus infection that most of its leaves are yellow- and black-
blotched by midsummer and the plant nearly defoliated
by autumn. Since nobody wants reminders of disease
and decay at his elbow, be sure to select varieties that
are specifically commended for their resistance to fungus spores.

Because plants in containers need constant attention
to watering, it isn't likely that people who take long
summer vacations will go in for extensive terrace plantings. For stay-at-homes, then, an important consideration is dependable summer flowering.

In sum, the criteria for selecting roses for container
growing are (1) satisfactory production of flowers
throughout the summer, (2) disease-resistant foliage and
(3) compact habit with canes clothed to the ground.
There are very few roses that can meet these exacting
standards, and even fewer when you recall that light-
colored varieties retain their effectiveness after sundown and should be the choice of those who enjoy outdoor dining and, afterwards, relaxing on the terrace to
watch fireflies cruise through the garden.

For profusion of bloom and compact habit, Floribundas are preeminent for container growing, either in individual pots, massed three to a larger tub or set in front of
Hybrid Teas to conceal their nonflowering lower canes.
The low-growing Polyanthas 'The Fairy' and 'Summer
Snow' meet the requirements to perfection. Planted at
the front of a tub or box, their decumbent canes would
droop over the rim, softening the rigid edge of the container and making an admirable soil cover. For especially choice spots, such as the pot-holding ring often
built under glass-topped tables, 'Cécile Brunner' would

**Fabergé**'s superb form makes it an ideal terrace companion.

contribute dense foliage and airy sprays of dainty flowers. If you have a wall fountain or pool, features that are often lined with soft turquoise blue, you could have no more charming accompaniment than a number of containers of 'Fabergé.' In addition to the cameo perfection of its form, 'Fabergé' has a delicate scent which some visitors liken to wild strawberries while others are reminded of the fragrance of sun-ripened peaches.

Among the Floribundas especially suited to container growing, the white 'Saratoga' stands high on the list. It is a moderately tall grower with fluttery clouds of semidouble flowers borne without pause all summer. 'Circus' with its lively change of colors would be a terrace companion of unfailing interest. 'City of Belfast,' fire orange to vermilion, has the valuable habit of sending out nearly horizontal branches from the base. These cover the soil and the rim of the container and make 'City of Belfast' of prime value for the forefront of a grouping. 'Matador,' deeper and even more dazzling than 'City of Belfast,' has a dense, neatly mounded habit, never leggy or straggly. 'City of Belfast' and 'Matador' are admittedly harsh in color and difficult to use, but if your porch furnishings are blue, green or yellow (anything but pink!), you can light the terrace with their brilliance. 'Courvoisier' is not a steady summer performer in hot climates and would not be admitted to this select list except for the scarcity of good yellow roses and its outstanding display in autumn.

Hybrid Teas have tall canes with all the flowers borne at their tips. When you are seated in a low chair, the nonblooming portion of the canes will be at eye level and therefore forced on your attention. The solution is to camouflage their shanks with Floribundas.

Some Hybrid Teas such as 'Peace' have excellent foliage and really need no borrowed petticoats. In addition to its melting beauty, 'Peace' has a dramatic life story that makes it a conversation piece as well as a superb decoration. In contrast to its name, 'Peace' had a stormy beginning. It first flowered for its breeder, Francis Meilland, in 1942, just as the German army of occupation was sweeping across France. M. Meilland recognized a treasure, named it for his mother, Mme. Antoine Meilland, and smuggled some budwood to the American consul as if it were the family jewels—which in the

event it proved to be. For the three years of the occupation, M. Meilland had no word of the fate of his rose.
When France was freed, M. Meilland learned that the
consul had indeed managed to get the precious budwood to the United States where it was enthusiastically
propagated—to the extent that when the delegates met
in San Francisco to frame the constitution of the United
Nations, their tables were furnished with bowls of the
rose. To honor the occasion, it was renamed 'Peace,' the
name by which it is known, bought, grown and loved by
millions of gardeners in this country.

The new yellow Hybrid Tea, 'New Day,' also has
splendid foliage. Like 'Peace' and other yellow roses, it
looks especially radiant when set before a rose-red brick
wall.

'Confidence,' 'Sierra Dawn' and 'Tiffany,' variously
pink or pink-and-yellow blends, have intense fragrance,
a ticket of admission to any seating area even if they
hadn't the added merit of sturdy growth and disease-free
foliage.

'Seashell' is a slow starter. It has taken several years
for it to settle in. It promises to be a rather small plant,
not exactly bursting with vigor but adequately clothed
with leaves. The flowers are also small but of a singularly
luminous shade of shrimp pink with touches of yellow,
especially attractive when seen with the sun behind it.
The moderate size of the plant, which might be a defect
in a large rose bed, is an asset in a container where compact habit is more valued than size.

'Pascali,' the white Hybrid Tea whose form is a standard of rose perfection, is especially beautiful when its
chiseled outline is set off by a dark background such as a
fence of cedar saplings or teak-stained louvered boards.

Since such fences are often used at the sides of a terrace to assure privacy or act as a windbreak, they can readily be adapted as a setting for groupings of roses.

An excellent way to display roses in containers is to set them on wooden benches in the shape of stepped-back ascending shelves at the base of a wall or fence. The Hybrid Teas, being tallest, would go on the upper shelf at the back, with intermediates such as Floribundas on the next lower shelf to hide the bare lower part of the HT's canes. The low-growing, wide-spreading varieties such as 'The Fairy' and 'Summer Snow' can be alternated with the Floribundas or set on duckboards on the floor.

Creating harmonious combinations is a stimulating test of artistry. If you are a beginner and not sufficiently familiar with rose colors to trust your judgment, here are some suggestions. In each case, the tallest variety is named first.

For soft pinks, try 'Pink Parfait,' 'Pinocchio' and 'The Fairy'; for a study in white, 'Pascali,' 'Saratoga' and 'Summer Snow.' A tawny yellow blend can be achieved with 'Apricot Nectar' or 'Mojave' behind 'Contempo,' and 'Golden Fleece' in front. If you want to bring in the incandescent fire-orange shades, use the tall buffy yellow 'Courvoisier' with 'City of Belfast' or 'Matador' in front. For lower masses in the gentler yellow-orange range, 'Circus' would pair charmingly with 'Golden Fleece.'

If you are an experienced rose grower, don't let these suggestions inhibit your invention. The beauty of growing roses in containers is that if you don't like the effect you first achieve, you can waltz them around until they meet your tastes.

A final note not directly concerned with rose growing, but one that will materially increase your enjoyment if you use your terrace after sundown: light it with hurricane lamps, not electricity. Lamps can be made in large numbers and with little expense by painting tuna fish cans flat black, centering in each one a chunky plumber's candle secured with melted wax, and finishing with the globe of a kerosene lamp. These lamps can be used not only on your dining table and to highlight any architectural feature such as a fountain but set quite close to flowering plants, though not directly under them (test with your hand for heat). If you are used to seeing your roses in strong sunlight, you will hardly believe the ethereal delicacy and romantic charm they gain under the spell of softly animated candle flames.

# Glossary

**Ball.** A defect of some full-petaled roses in which the outer petals become fused across the top of the bud and prevent its opening.

**Bud union.** The knob where bud joins understock.

**Button eye.** A ring of short petaloids with their tips held fast in the receptacle, forming a raised circlet around the center of a flower. For illustration, see the photograph of 'Stanwell Perpetual' on page 150.

**Guard petals.** Broad outer petals which encircle a mass of shorter petaloids.

**Mucro.** A needlelike point, sometimes hooked, at the distal end of a petal.

**Pelargonidin.** A brilliant orange-red pigment found in some geraniums (Pelargoniums) from which it takes its name.

**Quartering.** A quartered rose has its petals nested, each within a larger one, in distinct divisions. The heraldic Tudor rose is a stylized rendering of a quartered rose.

**Quill.** Roses are said to quill when the outer edges of their petals curl under, greatly reducing their breadth and resulting in a sharply pointed tip.

**Receptacle.** The expanded upper portion of a flower stalk from which proceed petals, sepals and reproductive organs. In roses, the receptacle matures to a fruit called a hip.

**Scion.** A bud or twig of a desired variety used in budding or grafting to an understock.

**Self-cleaning.** When spent flowers shed their petals promptly, they are said to be self-cleaning.

**Sepal.** The outermost series of floral parts, often green and leaflike.

**Sport.** A spontaneous mutation by which a new form appears asexually. A rose sport may result in a flower of different color from its parent or in climbing shoots developing from a bush rose.

**Trace elements.** Elements found in soils and plant tissues in minute quantities yet vital to the growth process. They include iron, boron, magnesium, calcium, sulphur, copper and zinc.

# Rose Buyer's Guide

The following listings are from 1978 catalogues unless otherwise noted. Only retail dealers that ship mail orders are included, on the assumption that if there is a local nursery where you can pick up rose plants, you would know about it. If anyone knows of sources for the varieties left blank by necessity, please notify the Librarian, Brooklyn Botanic Garden, 1000 Washington Avenue, Brooklyn, New York 11225, so that the catalogue file can be kept as informative as possible. We are especially eager to locate listings of 'Courvoisier,' 'Gay Princess,' 'Hallmark' and 'Sierra Dawn,' as these varieties are greatly admired and sought by visitors.

A      Armstrong Nurseries, Inc., P.O. Box 4060
Ontario, California 91761

ARP   Arp Roses, Inc., P.O. Box 6338
Tyler, Texas 75701

BUP   Burpee Seed Co.
Warminster, Pa. 18991

BUR   Burgess Seed & Plant Co. (1977)
Galesburg, Michigan 49053

CA    Carroll Gardens, 444 East Main Street
      Westminster, Maryland 21157

CO    C&O Nursery, 1700 North Wenachee Avenue
      Wenachee, Washington 98801

CP    Conard-Pyle Company
      West Grove, Pennsylvania 19390

DF    Dean Foster Nurseries
      Hartford, Michigan 49057

EM    Emlong Nurseries, Inc.
      Stevensville, Michigan 49127

FE    Fred Edmunds, 6235 S.W. Kahle Road
      Wilsonville, Oregon 97070

FO    Fowler's Nursery, 4210 Fayetteville Road (1977)
      Raleigh, North Carolina 27603

GU    Gurney Seed & Nursery Company
      Yankton, South Dakota 57079

IS    Inter-State Nurseries,
      Hamburg, Iowa 51644

JP    Jackson & Perkins Co.
      Medford, Oregon 97501

KE    Kelly Bros. Nurseries, Inc.
      Dansville, New York 14437

KR    Kroh Nurseries, Inc., P.O. Box 536
      Loveland, Colorado

KW    Kimbrew-Walter Roses, Route 1, Box 138-B
      Wills Point, Texas 75169

POT   P. O. Tate Nursery, Route 1, Box 307
      Tyler, Texas 75705

RH    Rose Hill Nursery, P.O. Box 495
      Minneapolis, Minnesota 55440

RM    Rocky Mountain Seed Co., 1325 15th Street
      Denver, Colorado 80217

RW    Roseway Nurseries, 8766 N.E. Sandy Boulevard
      Portland, Oregon 97220

ST    Stocking Rose Nursery, 785 N. Capital Avenue
      San Jose, California 95133

T     Tillotson's Roses, 802 Brown's Valley Road
      Watsonville, California 95076

TH    Thomasville Nurseries, Inc.
      Thomasville, Georgia 31792

TYT   Ty-Tex Rose Nurseries (1977)
      P.O. Box 532, Tyler, Texas 75710

WY    Wyant Roses, Johnny Cake Ridge,
      Mentor, Ohio 44060


'Agnes'  T
'Amélie Gravereaux'
'America'  A, ARP, BUP, BUR, CA, CO, CP, EM, FE, IS, JP,
    KR, KW, RH, RW, ST, TH, TYT, WY
'American Home'
'Angel Face'  A, ARP, CA, CP, EM, FE, FO, IS, KR, KW, POT,
    RH, RW, ST, TH, TYT, WY
'Apricot Nectar'  JP, RW, WY

'Bahia'  A, CA, CP, EM, FE, KR, POT, WY
'Baron Girod de l'Ain'  T
'Baroness Rothschild'  T
'Baronne Prevost'  T
'Belle de Crécy'  T
'Blanc Double de Coubert'  T
'Blaze'  A, ARP, BUR, CA, CO, CP, EM, IS, JP, KE, KR, KW,
    POT, RH, RM, RW, ST, TH, TYT, WY
'Bon Bon'  A, FE, IS, JP, KR, RH, RW, ST

'Cadenza'   A
'Captain Hayward'
'Captain Williams'
'Cathedral'   CA, CP, EM, FE, FO, IS, KR, RH, RM, RW, ST, WY
'Cécile Brunner'   KW, RW, ST, TH
'Chapeau de Napoléon'—see *R. centifolia cristata*
'Charisma'   A, ARP, BUP, CA, CO, CP, FE, IS, JP, KR, KW, POT, RM, RW, ST, TH, TYT
'Charlotte Armstrong'   A, ARP, DF, FE, FO, IS, KE, KR, KW, POT, RW, ST, TH, WY
'Chicago Peace'   ARP, BUP, BUR, CA, CP, FE, FO, IS, KR, KW, POT, RW, ST, TH, TYT, WY
'Chrysler Imperial'   A, ARP, BUP, BUR, CA, CO, CP, EM, FE, FO, IS, KE, KR, KW, POT, RH, RM, RW, ST, TH, TYT, WY
'Circus'   A, CP, DF, IS, KR, POT, RW, ST
'City of Belfast'   FE
'City of York'
'Common Moss'—see *R. centifolia muscosa*
'Comtesse de Murinais'   T
'Confidence'   BUR, CP, DF, FE, KW, POT, TH, WY
'Conrad Ferdinand Meyer'   WY
'Contempo'   A
'Courvoisier'
'Crimson Glory'   A, ARP, BUP, CA, CP, DF, FE, FO, G, IS, KR, KW, POT, RM, ST, T, TH, TYT

'Desiree Parmentier'
'Donald Prior'
'Don Juan'   A, ARP, BUP, BUR, CO, CP, DF, FE, IS, KE, KW, RM, RW, ST, TH, TYT, WY
'Double Delight'   A, ARP, BUP, BUR, CA, CO, CP, EM, FE, FO, IS, JP, KR, KW, POT, RM, RW, ST, TH, TYT, WY
'Duet'   A, FE, ST
'Dr. Eckener'   T

'Dr. Huey'
'Dr. W. Van Fleet'   T

'Eclipse,'   A, BUP, CP, DF, FE, FO, IS, KE, KW, POT, RW,
    ST, TH, TYT
'Eiffel Tower'   A
'Elegance'   T
'Eugenie Guinoisseau'
'Europeana'   A, ARP, BUR, CA, CO, CP, FE, IS, KW, POT,
    ST, TH, TYT, WY
'Evening Star'   JP

'Fabergé'   CA, FE, WY
'Fashion'   A, ARP, CA, CP, DF, FO, G, IS, KE, KW, POT, RH,
    RW, TH
'Ferdinand Pichard'   T
'Fire King'   CP
'Firelight'   KR, RM, WY
'First Edition'   A, ARP, BUP, BUR, CA, CO, CP, EM, FE, FO,
    G, IS, JP, KE, KW, POT, RM, RW, TH, TYT, WY
'First Love'   FE, RW, ST, T
'First Prize'   A, ARP, BUP, CA, CO, CP, EM, FE, FO, IS, JP,
    KR, KW, POT, RM, RW, ST, TH, TYT, WY
'Fisher Holmes'
'Floradora'   A, ARP, POT
'Fragrant Cloud'   A, CA, CP, FE, FO, JP, KR, KW, RH, RM,
    RW, ST, T, TH, WY
'Frau Karl Druschki'   A, POT, T, TH, TYT, WY
'Friendship'   ARP, CO, KW, RW, TH
'Frühlingsgold'

'Gay Princess'
'Gene Boerner'   A, CA, FE, IS, RW, ST, TYT, WY
'Général Jacqueminot'   T
'Gloire des Mousseux'   T
'Golden Fleece'   T

'Golden King'
'Golden Showers'    A, ARP, BUP, CA, CO, CP, FE, IS, KR,
    KW, POT, RH, RM, RW, TH, TYT, WY

'Hallmark'
'Hansa'    G, RH, T, WY
'Harison's Yellow'    RH, T, WY
'Heinrich Munch'    T
'Heirloom'    CA, JP, RW
'Helen Traubel'    A, ARP, CA, CP, DF, EM, FE, FO, IS, KE,
    KR, KW, POT, RW, ST, TH, WY

'Independence'
'Irish Mist'    FE
'Ivory Fashion'    CA, FE, KW, RM, ST, T

'John S. Armstrong'    A

'King's Ransom'    A, CA, CP, FE, IS, JP, KR, KW, POT, RW,
    ST, TH, TYT, WY
'Koenigin von Danemarck'    T, WY

'Lady X'    CA, CP, FE, KW, RM, RW, ST, WY
'Lemon Spice'    A
'Lowell Thomas'    A, ARP, BUR, DF, FO, G, IS, KE, KW, POT,
    RW, ST, WY

'Maiden's Blush'    T
'Ma Perkins'
'Marie Louise'
'Matador'    JP, KW
'Max Graf'
'Medallion'    A, CA, CO, CP, EM, FE, IS, JP, KR, KW, POT,
    RH, RW, ST, TH, TYT, WY
'Mirandy'    A, ARP, BUP, CA, CP, DF, EM, IS, KR, KW, POT,
    RH, RW, ST, TH, TYT, WY

'Mister Lincoln'  A, ARP, BUP, BUR, CA, CO, CP, EM, FE, FO, IS, KR, KW, POT, RH, RW, ST, TH, TYT, WY
'Mme. Charles Frederick Worth'
'Mme. Hardy'  T
'Mme. Louis Lévêque'  T, WY
'Mojave'  A, CA, CO, EM, FE, G, IS, KR, KW, POT, RW, ST, TYT, WY
'Montezuma'  A, CA, CP, DF, IS, KR, KW, POT, RH, RW, ST, TH, TYT
'Mousseux Ancien'—see *R. centifolia muscosa*

'New Day'  JP, KR, KW, ST
'New Dawn'  A, CA, DF, TH, WY
'Nova Zembla'

'Oklahoma'  A, CA, CO, CP, FE, KR, ST, TH, WY
'Oratam'
'Oregold'  A, ARP, BUP, BUR, CA, CO, CP, EM, FE, FO, IS, JP, KR, KW, POT, RH, RM, RW, ST, TH, WY

'Paradise'  JP, KR, ST, WY
'Pascali'  A, BUR, CA, CP, FE, KR, KW, POT, RW, ST, TH, WY
'Peace'  A, ARP, BUP, BUR, CA, CO, CP, DF, EM, FE, FO, G, IS, JP, KE, KR, KW, POT, RH, RW, ST, TH, TYT, WY
'Perfume Delight'  A, ARP, BUP, CA, CO, CP, EM, FE, FO, HW, POT, RH, RM, RW, ST, TH, TYT, WY
'Pink Bountiful'
'Pink Grootendorst'  G, T, WY
'Pink Parfait'  A
'Pinocchio'  EM, KE, KR, POT, RW, TYT
'Pristine'  JP, KR, ST, WY
'Proud Land'  JP, KR, POT, WY

'Queen Elizabeth'  A, BUR, CA, CO, CP, DF, EM, FO, IS, KE, KW, POT, RH, RM, RW, ST, TH, TYT, WY

'Red Chief'
'Redgold'   A, ARP, CA, CO, CP, EM, FE, IS, JP, KR, RW, ST, TH, TYT, WY
'Red Grootendorst'   G, RH, RW, T, WY
'Red Masterpiece'   BUR, CA, JP, KW, WY
'Red Pinocchio'   ARP, DF, EM, FO, IS, KE, KR, KW, POT, TH, TYT
'Reine des Violettes'   T
'Roger Lambelin'   T
'Rosa Mundi'—see *R. gallica versicolor*
'Roserie de l'Hay'   T
'Royal Canadian'   RW, TH
'Ruskin'   T

## ROSA

*Rosa centifolia cristata*   T
*R. c. muscosa* ('Common Moss')   T
*R. damascena bifera*   T
*R. d. versicolor* ('York and Lancaster')
*R. foetida*
*R. f. bicolor*   RW, WY
*R. gallica officinalis*   T
*R. gallica versicolor*   ('Rosa Mundi')
*R. hugonis*   KE, T, WY
*R. multiflora*   EM
*R. roxburghii*
*R. rugosa albo-plena*
*R. r. rubra*   EM, G, KE, T, WY
*R. spinosissima altaica*
*R. wichuraiana*


'Salet'   T
'Saratoga'   CP, KR, RW, ST, WY
'Scarlet Knight'   A, CA, CP, KR, POT, RW, ST, TH, TYT, WY
'Seashell'   A, ARP, BUP, BUR, CA, CP, EM, FE, FO, IS, JP, KR, KW, POT, RH, RM, RW, ST, TH, TYT, WY
'Sierra Dawn'
'Silver Moon'

'Sir Thomas Lipton'
'Snowfire'    BUR, JP, KR, KW, POT, RM, RW, ST, TH, WY
'Soeur Thérèse'
'Soleil d'Or'
'Song of Paris'    A
'Spartan'    A, CA, CP, DF, IS, KR, KW, POT, RW, TH, TYT, WY
'Speaker Sam'
'Spellbinder'    CA
'Stanwell Perpetual'    T
'Sterling Silver'    A, BUP, CA, EM, IS, JP, RW, ST, TH
'Summer Snow'    ARP, KW, POT, TH, TYT
'Summer Sunshine'    A, CP, FE, KW, POT, RW, ST, TH, TYT,
    WY
'Sutter's Gold'    A, ARP, BUP, CA, CO, FE, G, IS, KR, RW, ST,
    TH, WY

'Tempo'    JP, KW, WY
'The Fairy'    CA, CP, FE, FO, G, IS, KE, RW, ST, T, TH, WY
'Tiffany'    A, ARP, BUR, CA, CP, DF, EM, FE, IS, KR, KW,
    POT, RW, ST, TH, TYT, WY
'Tropicana'    A, ARP, BUP, CA, CO, CP, FE, FO, IS, JP, KR,
    KW, POT

'Ulrich Brunner'

'Vanguard'
'Vierge de Cléry' ('Unique Blanche')

'White Masterpiece'    FE, JP, KR, KW, WY
'Will Scarlet'    T, WY

'Yankee Doodle'    A, ARP, BUP, BUR, CA, CP, EM, FE, FO,
    IS, KR, KW, POT, RH, ST, TH, WY
'York and Lancaster'—see R. damascena versicolor

# INDEX

# INDEX

*Page numbers for illustrations are in italics.*